Helen Waddell's
WRITINGS FROM JAPAN

Edited and introduced by

DAVID BURLEIGH

IRISH ACADEMIC PRESS
DUBLIN • PORTLAND, OR

First published in 2005 by
IRISH ACADEMIC PRESS
44 Northumberland Road, Dublin 4, Ireland

and in the United States of America by
IRISH ACADEMIC PRESS
c/o ISBS, Suite 300
920 NE 58th Avenue
Portland, Oregon 97213-3644

Website: **www.iap.ie**

British Library Cataloguing in Publication Data
A catalogue entry is available on application

ISBN 0-7165-2795-2 (cloth)
ISBN 0-7165-3350-2 (paper)

Library of Congress Cataloging-in-Publication Data
A catalog entry is available on application

Typeset by FiSH Books, London
Printed by MPG Books, Bodmin, Cornwall

Helen Waddell's
WRITINGS FROM JAPAN

‘Still to my brother turns, with ceaseless pain,
And drags at each remove a lengthening chain.’

Oliver Goldsmith, *The Traveller**

* Quoted by Helen Waddell in a letter to her sister in the 1930s.

Contents

Illustrations

Preface

At the height of her fame in the 1930s, the Irish medieval scholar Helen Waddell (1889–1965) was known, in Dublin, as 'Ulster's darling'. Her classic study of medieval Latin poets, *The Wandering Scholars*, its companion volume *Mediaeval Latin Lyrics*, and the novel *Peter Abelard* had brought her not only honour in academe, but popularity with the reading public too. That the rhythms of her brilliantly evocative prose reflected an Irish background, many of her readers would have recognised, but fewer would have understood the influence exerted on her imagination by the East. Waddell's best-known books are now receiving critical examination elsewhere: what this volume aims to gather and explore are her less-known early writings on Japan, where she had been born. It is a subject that she drew on only in the 1910s, and which her later writing has substantially obscured. Yet it is evident from her letters that Waddell once considered assembling a book of her writings on Japan. Such of these writings as remain have been collected here.

The Waddell family's background in Japan has, of course, been known about by scholars for some time, if not investigated in much detail. It was shared by one of Helen's older brothers, Samuel Waddell (1878–1967), better known as the playwright Rutherford Mayne, and is discussed in a recent edition of Mayne's plays, edited by Wolfgang Zach (2000). The first reference to this background in Helen's case came from the editor of a posthumous book of children's stories, Eileen Colwell, and, indeed, the title story of this collection, *The Princess Splendour and Other Stories* (1969), was taken from Japan. The matter did not, however, receive much attention in the first book-length account of Waddell's life, *The Mark of the Maker: A Memoir of Helen Waddell* by Monica Blackett (1973). It was not until the second biographical account, *Helen Waddell: A Biography* by Dame Felicitas Corrigan, appeared in 1986, that much detail about Waddell's early life was furnished from unpublished manuscript material. It was the latter volume, which is almost twice the length of its predecessor, that supplied the leads and inspiration for the present study, which concentrates entirely on Japan.

The writings themselves consist of some autobiographical stories (four completed stories and a fragment); three imaginary tales that mix legendary events with realistic settings, and the two-act play into which one of these was then extended; and two densely allusive literary essays. Some, though not all, of these pieces were published (or, in the case of the play, performed) not long after they were written, and where relevant, details have been given. All have been checked against surviving manuscript and typescript copies. The three sections of the book are intended to indicate the different types of writing they contain, but the order is also more or less chronological in terms of composition. The changes in style and content show, among other things, Waddell's development as an author. Though none of these works is unsophisticated, it is the last of them that most nearly approaches what was to become Waddell's mature scholarly style and anticipates her brilliant debut in the 1920s. Despite their diversity of form and content, these pieces are not simply fugitive writings connected by the subject of Japan, for there is also a biographical strand, which is explored in the Introduction, that can be found to draw them all together.

The biographical background Waddell supplies herself from her correspondence. In addition to her frequent letters to her older sister Margaret, Helen also wrote weekly to Dr George Taylor, a missionary in India, from 1915 until his death. Most of the Waddell papers are stored in the library of Stanbrook Abbey, a Benedictine monastery on the outskirts of Worcester in England, and I have drawn extensively on this collection. Many of Waddell's letters to her sister are undated, but dates can often be ascribed to them based on their contents. Most of the letters Waddell wrote to Taylor have survived, though only a few of those he wrote to her have done so. The majority of these letters can be accurately dated, though there are a few to which dates still cannot be ascribed precisely. All the correspondence for this period held at Stanbrook, with the exception of Taylor's letters, has been filed under the heading 'CA', for Cedar Avenue, the place in Belfast where it was written. Most of the letters have been numbered, but only the dates will be given when they are quoted here. Without Helen Waddell's own comments in her letters, especially those she wrote to her sister and to Taylor, it would be almost impossible to understand her early preoccupation with Japan.

George Pritchard Taylor (1855–1920) was a third-generation missionary who had been born in the west of India and grew up speaking Gujarati, which he could read and write fluently. He had attended a missionary school in London and then grammar school in Belfast, where he went on to distinguish himself at the university. He received an MA with first-class honours there in 1874, was licensed to preach the gospel two years later and returned to India in 1877 with his new wife, who was also a missionary. Thereafter Taylor went back to Ireland only twice, on furlough in 1890 and again in 1914. Some information about his background, which was originally English, can be found in *The Indian Mission of the Irish Presbyterian Church* by the Revd. Robert Jeffrey (1890). The missionary work of Irish Presbyterians seems to have been confined to the western provinces of India. At the time Helen Waddell knew Taylor he was the principal of a divinity college for native pastors, Stevenson College in Ahmedabad. Further information about him can be gleaned from missionary journals. Waddell's other important exchange of letters at this time, with Professor George Saintsbury (1845–1933), the literary critic, yields little with regard to Japan. The surviving letters exchanged between Waddell and Saintsbury are stored in the library of Queen's University in Belfast.

It is Waddell's correspondence with her older sister Margaret, to whom as we know she was very close, that provides the most valuable insights into private relations within the family. These letters are of particular interest regarding their brother Billy, who features strongly in Helen's writings on Japan. Margaret's teenage diary, written in Japan at the close of the nineteenth century, further enhances our understanding, not only because it offers a portrait of Helen as a child, but also because it is replete with details of the family's daily life. The diary, which is also kept at Stanbrook, is handwritten in a thick notebook and the pages are unnumbered, but the entries are all dated. Quotations from it can be easily identified by their dates of entry, and that is how they are given here. In order to maintain the flavour of the original document, I have retained Margaret's own spelling and punctuation, without correction, even where there were obvious mistakes. The same applies to the diarist's occasional use of words from Japanese, which modern orthography requires to be italicised or underlined. All the Japanese words in the diary are in roman letters. Similarly, in the stories and essays by Helen Waddell, while some attention has been given to discrepancies between the different published and unpublished versions, the older style has been preserved. This includes certain irregularities which were characteristic of the author and the time at which she was writing.

Readers familiar with other writings about Helen Waddell may find it curious that I refer to her older sister as 'Margaret' instead of 'Meg', the name she was generally known by in her adult life. The reason for this is partly to be more objective, but mainly to avoid a separation of the adult from the child. All the Waddell children seem to have been called by different pet or shortened names at different times. Margaret, for example, seems to have been 'Maggie' as a child (the name she gives on the cover of her diary) and Meg as an adult, though Helen refers to her also occasionally as 'Peg' or 'Peggy'. Helen herself never seems to have had another name, but she uses a wide range of pet names and affectionate diminutives for herself and other family members in her letters. I have preferred, for the sake of consistency, the plainer forms. The exception to this is William Waddell, one of the younger brothers, whom I refer to generally as 'Billy', since that is the way that Helen refers to him not only in her letters, but more importantly in the autobiographical stories in which he figures. Again the reason is consistency since, although this single exception may seem baffling, I believe it improves the cogency of the discussion, which must deal simultaneously with the children's real life and Helen's fictional representation of it.

Additional, albeit rather spare, information about Billy's life, and death, has been extracted from the records of Campbell College in Belfast, the archives of the Royal College of Surgeons in Edinburgh, and the shipping records in the Public Record Office at Kew. For the family's background in Japan I have drawn on the published proceedings of two large conferences of Protestant missionaries to Japan, held there in 1883 and 1900, besides the more general histories of missionary work. These documents are in English, but the most extensive references to Hugh Waddell, Helen's father, are contained in documents in Japanese, mainly the historical records of institutions to which he was connected. The records of Meiji Gakuin, of which Hugh was a staff member when it was founded, proved particularly useful, since they furnished, among other things, the address at which the Waddell family was most likely living when Helen was born. Japanese personal names are given in the customary fashion, with the family name first, unless otherwise indicated. The original spellings of all Japanese words have been retained and more modern ones confined to annotations. Arabian and Chinese names are likewise given, in terms of both order and spelling, as they appear in the original writings.

In the preparation of this book I have incurred numerous debts, both large and small. My first debt is to the pioneering work done by Waddell's biographer, Dame Felicitas Corrigan, OSB, who welcomed me at Stanbrook when first I went there to seek advice. On subsequent visits to examine the papers, I have always been treated hospitably and helped by the nuns at Stanbrook, especially by Dame Philippa Edwards. I am deeply grateful to them. In my first gathering of manuscript material, I was also greatly assisted by Waddell's relatives, particularly by her niece Miss Mollie Martin, who was generous in sharing her recollections of her aunt, and has been thoroughly supportive throughout, kindly granting permission to reproduce all the work appearing here. Martin Waddell, Helen's grand-nephew and himself an author of distinction, also assisted my investigations. I owe much to Professor Norman Vance of the University of

Sussex, who supervised my thesis on these writings, and to Dr Jennifer FitzGerald, formerly of the Queen's University in Belfast, both of whom are Waddell scholars. The staff of the Queen' s University library, above all Mary Kelly, besides the staff of the Linenhall Library, the Presbyterian Historical Association, Assembly College, Campbell College, and Victoria College, all in Belfast, also gave me important practical assistance. Beyond these institutions, I was well served, in Ireland, by the staff in the library at the University of Ulster at Coleraine, and at the Public Record Office of Northern Ireland; in mainland Britain, by those at the British Museum Reading Room (now the British Library) in London, the Public Record Office at Kew, and the Royal College of Surgeons in Edinburgh; and, in the United States, by those at the New York City Public Library.

In Japan, I have been well assisted by the librarians at Waseda Umversity in Tokyo, at Kansai University in Osaka, and at Ferris University in Yokohama, during my investigations. I am particularly grateful to Nakayama Kazuko in the records office at Ferris for helping me to clarify many of the details of the missionary background, and for locating sources in Japanese. Through her, I was able to make further reference to records at Meiji Gakuin, and her help in understanding these was invaluable. There is not space to detail all the help and support that I received from friends and relatives, but I should like to mention four by name: Note Osamu and Joseph O'Leary helped me to locate and understand Japanese and German texts respectively, while my brother-in-law, Andrew Jaggers, gave me advice about shipping matters; finally, Michael Lamb, my old friend and mentor from the University of Ulster, and a distinguished authority on things Japanese, provided me with a quiet room and the use of a computer so that I could finish the book. My editors at the Irish Academic Press have been helpful and patient in seeing the results into print, but any errors that remain are necessarily my own responsibility.

Acknowledgement is made to Constable and Robinson for permission to reproduce 'Flowers and Moonlight on the Spring River' from Arthur Waley's book *One Hundred & Seventy Chinese Poems*. The author has endeavoured to gain permission from all sources regarding permissions for this book.

Lastly I should like to dedicate this collection to my mother, my sister and my brother, all of whom have, at different times, been to Kamakura with me; but most of all to the memory of my father, who never had the chance.

DB
Tokyo 2002

Introduction

'The richest thing in my life has been Japan,' wrote the Irish scholar Helen Waddell to an older correspondent while still a young woman in her twenties. The recipient of the letter, Dr George P. Taylor, was a Presbyterian missionary to India, as Waddell's own father had been to Japan at the time that she was born. Her childhood experience of that country reveals itself in the Japanese subject matter that permeates her early writing. At the same time, it is clear that the adult author's developing imagination had been enriched in ways other than simply by the exotic experience of a far-off land. This is indicated by the rider that she added to this statement in her letter: 'The richest thing in my life has been Japan – outside books, I mean.'

Helen Waddell's relation with Japan resulted solely from the fact that her father chose to go there as a missionary. Hugh Waddell (1840–1901)[1] came from an old County Down family which had extensive clerical connections. His own father, also called Hugh, was for many years minister of the Presbyterian church at Glenarm in County Antrim. The younger Hugh was first sent to an apprenticeship in business, however, and it was only after he had served a few years of this that his spiritual calling was awoken. It happened during the great religious awakening of 1859, when an evangelical fervour swept across the north of Ireland. Though already 19 years of age, Hugh then began to study to enter college, for which he undertook preparatory work at the Belfast Royal Academical Institution. He entered the Queen's University of Belfast in 1862, gained a BA degree with honours and, after further study at the Presbyterian Assembly College, was licensed to preach the gospel in 1868. Though his first call was to his father's congregation at Glenarm, the younger Hugh had set his heart on missionary work. The Mission Board, to whom he had offered his services, asked him to go out to China.

Hugh Waddell's service in the north-eastern part of China began in 1869, but was curtailed by illness, which forced him to return to Ireland in 1871. Once he had recovered, rather than being sent back to the

East, he was asked by the Mission Board to reopen its mission in Spain, to which he went in 1872. He was accompanied by his wife Jane ('Jenny'), and this is where their first child and eldest son was born. However, Hugh did not find much satisfaction in this work, in a country that was already Christian, and still retained a strong desire to 'preach the Gospel to the heathen'. When he discovered that the United Presbyterian Church of Scotland required a missionary to Japan, he offered his services to them and was accepted. He resigned from his post in Spain in 1874 and prepared to join two other missionaries from the Scottish church who had departed for the East a few months earlier. The Waddells finally reached Japan on 10 June 1874.

Revd Hugh Waddell.

The land in which Hugh Waddell and his wife arrived, not only as missionaries but also in some sense as pioneers, had not long been opened to the West. During the Edo period (1603–1867), when Japan was almost completely isolated from the outside world, Christianity had been proscribed under penalty of death. After the country had been forced open by the United States for the purposes of trade in 1853, a period of vigorous and sometimes violent change ensued, during which the Shogunate was dismantled and the Emperor restored to formal power. In 1868, when the Restoration was completed, the Emperor's residence was moved from the old capital Kyoto to the largest city Edo, where he began to occupy the former Shogun's castle. Edo was renamed 'Tokyo' (literally 'East Capital') and declared the seat of government, and the new era thus officially began. With the dispersal of the clans, the foundations were laid for a parliamentary form of government, and the eventual transformation of the country from a militaristic, feudal state, to a democratic modern one. Religious freedom was not immediately guaranteed, but changes were gradually taking place. '[E]arly in 1873', as one historian explains it, 'the edict against Christianity was removed from public notice boards. This did not in theory change the law, but it meant that the government did not intend to enforce it.'[2] It was a hopeful, if uncertain, situation.

In the absence of an established framework for their activities, the first task of missionaries was to establish contact with local communities. This was achieved mainly through their work in the fields of medicine and education, by setting up dispensaries and schools. Since travel in the interior was still restricted, these activities were at first confined to the cities in which Westerners were permitted to reside. In Tokyo, where Hugh was to be based, the Japanese government had created a special foreign settlement, in the Tsukiji district to the east of the castle.[3] It was in this district, adjacent to the bay and bordered by canals, that he started work, teaching at a college there. In January 1876 he opened a school of his own for boys in the western part of the city, and the trust and goodwill achieved by this venture led to the establishment of a small church. The way was evidently prepared by informal preaching, and one visitor to Japan describes Hugh at work in 1877, undoubtedly, from the narrow streets, somewhere in the heart of Tokyo:

> Late in the evening we closed a very happy day by accompanying our host, one of the kindest-hearted and most self-denying of mission workers, to his final service. What we lost in China through Mr. Waddell's ill-health, Japan has abundantly gained. It is rather a free talk than a service, and is held in a low room that opens off a crowded and, as usual, narrow street. A lamp hung above the door bears on one of its sides an invitation to enter. The room could hold about sixty people. They squatted on the matted floor as they entered – men from their work (for except in Government offices there is no Sabbath in Japan), and women with children at the breast. They filled up all the space, and then a crowd of figures, just visible through the semi-darkness, filled up all the space about the door. Some would move away, but

> others always took their place. First the catechist spoke, and then the missionary. All listened, though in the gloom there could sometimes be seen little but the sparkle of dark eyes. One old man of eighty-two, clearly seen under the light of the lamp, was absorbed and happy. He had been a physician and a keen student of Confucius, and after a struggle had yielded to Christ, and was baptised the Sabbath previous.[4]

The church, which was consecrated in the spring of 1879, was located at Fukide-chō, Azabu-ku, an address no longer in existence.[5] Hugh's first tiny congregation consisted of eighteen men, eight women and three children. Before long he started out-station work in other parts of the country as well, partly making use of boys who had studied at his school, while the church in Tokyo was overseen by the assistant he had trained. After approximately ten years in Japan, Waddell returned to Ireland on furlough, by which time he and his wife already had several more children of their own.

The nine remaining Waddell children were all born in Tokyo, and, since most of them were boys, it is not surprising that their father should have been particularly interested in boys' education. But, apart from brief mentions in an early summary of missionary work,[6] no record of the school survives, which suggests that it may have been a short-lived or unsuccessful venture.[7] The Scottish Presbyterian Church, under whose sponsorship Hugh had come to Japan, had a fairly small representation there compared with some of the other Protestant denominations. In 1877 it joined forces with the American Presbyterian Church and the American Reformed (Dutch) Church, as the United Church of Christ in Japan. Though 'United' was later dropped, the unification of the denominations held. The 1880s brought a rapid increase in the number of converts to all churches, as part of the general enthusiasm for Westernisation at that time. The year that Helen Waddell was born, 1889, saw the promulgation of a new constitution and the completion of the railway link between Tokyo and Kyoto. The next year, 1890, the parliamentary form of government which had been outlined in the constitution and discussed for several years before, finally came into operation.

Since Helen was the tenth and last of the children (and one of only two girls), it is probable that some of her older brothers had already left Japan before her birth. When they reached the age of ten or so, the Waddell boys were sent back 'home' to Ireland, usually in pairs, to finish their education. We do not know exactly how many of them still remained in Japan at the end of the 1880s. Nor do we know precisely where the family was living when each of them was born, since, although the births were presumably registered at the British Embassy, most of its records were destroyed in the fires that

Jane ('Jenny') Waddell with her ten children. Helen is on her mother's lap, and Billy is on the bottom right.

followed the Great Kantō Earthquake in 1923. An address for the family residence can, however, be established for the late 1880s, since at that time Hugh became a staff member of a newly-established school for boys, Meiji Gakuin in Tokyo. The school was set up in 1886 and the letters of registration give his address,[8] and show this to be have been adjacent to Fukide-chō, where he had previously lived and had a church. The church had moved to a more central location under a native pastor in 1883,[9] but the Waddell family continued to live in the same neighbourhood apparently.

Hugh Waddell was a scholar of some distinction and belonged to the committee appointed in 1876 to translate the Bible into Japanese, though it is unclear how much he actually contributed to this work.[10] He took a strong interest in the debate then current about the best way to translate the names of the triune God into Japanese, favouring the term *ki* over the more generally accepted *rei* for the Holy Spirit. He explained his preference in terms of the Chinese characters with which these words were written and the nuanced differences in meaning. Hugh's knowledge of such matters derived in part from his early study of Chinese during the period of service he spent in north China. What he had learnt then would have greatly assisted his study of Japanese, the written form of which makes extensive use of

Chinese characters. One of Hugh's published papers offers a detailed comparison of Christian and Confucian thought,[11] and his learning on this subject would undoubtedly have impressed the elderly Confucian gentleman described above. Many Chinese characters are quoted in the text of the paper and the rhythmic quality of the prose in which it is written suggests someone with a gift for oratory. Indeed, the author is credited with having been 'a ready debater, and … much sought after for sermons and lectures, both in English and Japanese.'[12] It is important to observe, however, that the Scottish Presbyterians were few in number compared with their American counterparts and, whatever their individual distinction, would inevitably have been somewhat marginalised by them.

There is a considerable literature in which the foreign residents of nineteenth-century Japan recount their experiences of the country and record the changes taking place in it.[13] From the accounts of diplomats, missionaries and travellers it is possible to gain some impression of the kind of life that the Waddell family lived.[14] As a counterpoint to the reverent histories that the missionaries in particular wrote about themselves, it is worth noting a less respectful incidental portrait of one of them provided by the British novelist and poet Rudyard Kipling (1865–1936). Kipling visited Japan as a young man in 1889 and again in 1892, dates which encompass Helen Waddell's infancy there. He wrote two series of letters about the country designed for publication in newspapers. As he left for America after the first visit in 1889, he observed his fellow passengers:

> The missionaries are perhaps the queerest portion of the cargo. Did you ever hear an English minister sit down and lecture for half an hour on the freight-traffic receipts and general working of, let us say, the Midland? The Professor [his companion] has been sitting at the feet of a keen-eyed, close-bearded, swarthy man who expounded unto him kindred mysteries with a fluency and precision that a city leader-writer might have envied. 'Who's your financial friend with the figures at his fingers' ends?' I asked. 'Missionary – Presbyterian Mission to the Japanese', said the Professor. I laid my hand upon my mouth and was dumb.[15]

Even allowing for humorous exaggeration and the fact that the author was not very sympathetic to missionary endeavour, this sketch nevertheless suggests that the (in this case American) missionaries were sometimes rather brisk and businesslike in their approach.

An entertaining and useful subjective portrait of life in Tokyo at the time that Helen Waddell was born may be found in the diary of Clara A.N. Whitney (1860–1936), a member of the American Presbyterian Church who was undoubtedly known to the Waddells. Clara Whitney arrived in Japan in 1875, a girl of 14 accompanying her father, who had been invited to set up a commercial college. Though at first priggish and disdainful, she soon became completely fluent in the language and eventually married a Japanese man, to whom she bore five children. The Whitney family were considerably benefited when, on the occasion of the father's early dismissal from the college, they came under the protection of a wealthy and influential Japanese, Katsu Kaishū (1823–99), and it was one of his children Clara married. She returned to the United States permanently, with her children but without her husband, in 1900. Her published diary covers the years 1875–87.[16]

There is some coincidence between the names that occur in Clara's diary and that of Helen's older sister Margaret, written at a later date. Margaret's diary contains some references to the Whitney family, and we know that they attended the same church. Clara's circumstances would have been more comfortable, owing to her father-in-law's position. The Waddell family may have experienced occasional hardship, in part at least from the expense of educating so many children, but they were not particularly poor. Indeed, the missionaries were sometimes envied by the other foreigners, presumably because their income was assured and not dependent on the vagaries of trade. In 1891 (or 1892), however, when Helen was still a small child, it was decided that the Waddell family would travel back to Ireland. The mother and children made the journey first, and, shortly after their arrival, Jane Waddell died of typhoid. The three-year-old Helen then contracted the disease and became dangerously ill. It seems that her late-arriving and desperate father was able to revive his infant daughter only by speaking to her in Japanese.[17] When she had recovered and the family were settled, he was obliged to return to his work in Japan, which he did at the end of 1893.

It was in Japan that the Waddells were reunited in 1895. Hugh, who had married his cousin in order to have someone to care for his youngest children, had gone out first and waited for them to follow. He stayed at least part of the time with colleagues in the brick-built, foreign concession that the Japanese government had erected to accommodate Western residents in central Tokyo.[18] When the arrival of his wife and children was imminent, he arranged housing for them, once more in the western part of the city. The centre of Tokyo was traditionally located to the east, on flat land by the rivers, but many of the foreigners favoured the green and hilly region to the west. A contemporary guidebook describes the Azabu district, where the Waddells lived, as one of 'the highest and healthiest parts of Tokyo'.[19] This time it was only the four youngest children who accompanied their stepmother back to Japan. By the middle of the 1890s, however, the future for missionaries there had become less bright and certain.

The changes had begun to set in at the beginning of the decade, even before the Waddells left. The Rescript on Education issued in the Emperor's name in 1890, though ambiguously worded, encouraged greater loyalty to the state. While there can be no doubt that the missionaries had a great and enduring influence on areas such as education, loyalty to institutions such as churches was undermined by this directive, and membership declined as a result. Considerable numbers of converts had been won in the 1880s, but this went into rapid retreat. The issue of perhaps greatest concern to the nation in the 1890s was that of extraterritoriality. When the country was first opened up to trade, foreign residents had been granted extraterritorial rights, according to which they were not subject to Japanese law, in the treaty ports to which their activities were initially restricted. When the new constitution came into effect the time seemed to have arrived to end this privileged arrangement, which was humiliating to the Japanese. Treaties with the Western powers were therefore renegotiated and extraterritorial rights gradually removed, though the new arrangements did not come into full effect until 1899. Externally Japan had begun to reassert itself as well, in the short but successful Sino-Japanese War of 1894–95.

It was to these much less encouraging circumstances that Hugh Waddell returned with his wife and children, to recommence his missionary

A studio portrait, taken in Japan, of the four youngest Waddell children with their father and stepmother. Left to right: Billy, Margaret, George, Hugh, Martha, Helen.

endeavour. The youngest children – Margaret, William Rutherford, George Frederick and Helen Jane – had been born at two-year intervals – in 1883, 1885, 1887 and 1889, respectively. The family settled in the same area that they had lived in before and Hugh resumed his work with the Church of Christ, though in precisely what capacity we do not know. An estrangement seems to have taken place some time after his return between him and the other members of the United Church of Christ, causing him to withdraw. The point of contention appears to have been that Hugh felt the Synod had dealt with the expressed criticisms of a native pastor with undue severity. He joined instead an open-air mission run independently in Ueno Park and began preaching regularly there. This mission was organised by a Miss Kate Youngman, an American missionary.[20] Throughout his career Hugh seems to have been much in demand as a preacher, and we may take it that he spoke in English when he addressed a mainly foreign congregation. But evangelising work had necessarily to be done in Japanese. There is a delightful description, among the Waddell papers, of Hugh preaching out of doors in Ueno Park. Its exact provenance is not known but it was evidently written in English by a Japanese observer or written in Japanese and afterwards translated:

> On Sunday afternoon I went out from my house to take a walk. It was in early spring. The North Wind was blowing cold when I arrived at Uyeno [Ueno] Park. There were few abroad in the Park. I rested under an old oak tree. Whilst I was resting I heard a voice in the distance. Looking round to see where the sound came from, I found the voice to be of Mr. Waddell, the Park Lecturer. He was preaching close to a tea-house. As it was a long time since I last heard him I went forward to listen. The audience consisted at first of about 14 or 15 people, some apprentices, some nurse-girls, also gentlemen and merchants. The pulpit was a little way from the road, near to it were two benches under the oak tree covered with mats. Behind Mr. Waddell stood a small organ, at his left a signboard which bears an inscription written thus –
>
> *A Lecture on Christianity*, by Mr. Waddell and Mr. Shinawara.
>
> on his right a stand on which was placed a sheet of music containing the hymn to be sung. There were two men beside him who seem very cold as they sat on the bench. This completes the arrangements for the lecture.
>
> The robe of Mr. Waddell was a frock coat as usual his necktie was black and broad. He looks to be of the age of sixty: his hair is white as snow, his face as red as ink: his countenance differs from the ordinary

European, his face is flat: nose is not high: eyes partially hidden by the eyelids: his eyes are glittering under the over-arching eyebrows. No one can look at his eyes without being impressed by a feeling of reverence. The man resembles in appearance the statue of Socrates. An historian told us Socrates was not handsome: neither is Mr. Waddell; but his countenance and his zeal and earnestness in preaching like to Socrates is a strange coincidence. If we can induce another point to the resemblance already noted it must be said that Mr. Waddell deserves to be reverenced as the Sage or Socrates of this day.

I feel sorry the number of the audience was so small. Notwithstanding this he however was preaching as sincerely and earnestly with his curious Japanese as if he were preaching to an audience of hundreds of thousands. As I stood there the sermon was half over. His tall figure growing more solemn, his strong voice more clear, looking up to heaven he pointed up to the top of the oak tree and said 'What is it makes the large tree grow? It is the heat and light of the sun. Nothing but sun can make it grow. A hibachi* or an andon** cannot make it grow. If we wish to make a noble man, God is necessary. Idols and Buddhist priests are of no use – what is absolutely needful is God in heaven.' When he said this two or three spectacled young men standing behind me said in low voice 'His grammar is not correct.' 'No foreigner can use properly the particles in Japanese grammar…' 'But he is very honest.' 'We must go.' … 'Wait a little, let us hear him longer…' Mr. Waddell went on with skilled gestures and postures with his sermon. 'A parent protects his children, and behold young boys who come up to Tokio away from their parents do not study diligently, drink wine and go to bad places. They become degraded, simply because their parents cannot protect them.' The hearers all at once laughed a little because of his curious illustration. 'The same reason those who do not believe in God act badly, gamble and steal, but those who believe in God are protected by God: therefore they are kept in the right way. God can see in the dark. God is to be feared.' At this time the number of the audience increased. At first the number of the audience was about fifteen, but it increased more and more so that I who was in the outer circle at first found myself soon so surrounded as to be in the inner part of the circle. Some people passed on, others came, and still the audience increased. Mr. Waddell said moreover 'Christ took upon him the sins of his people. He answered for them, became their surety. A parent answers

* *Hibachi*, a brazier or firebox, half-filled with burning charcoal and ashes.

** *Andon*, an oil lamp covered with a round or square paper shade, for indoor use, especially at night.

for his child, an emperor is responsible for his people. When China was defeated the man sent by China with proposals of peace – a German – was repulsed, because of his imperfect qualification. Next came A Cho in Kaii. He also was repulsed for the same reason. At last came Li Hung Chang. The Japanese government recognized him because he was the supreme officer of the Chinese court. He made peace for his nation. Christ redeemed the sins of the people of the whole world. Christ is sinless, Christ is the parent of his people – an affectionate parent.' The audience was as quiet as the earth after rainfall.

Mr. Waddell after ten more minutes suddenly changed his tone and lifting high his Bible he said 'Men must trust upon God. Those who would trust in God must read this book.' These words were the conclusion of his sermon. He then awkwardly bowed his body and saluted the audience. He descended from the pulpit. The semi-circular multitude began to move but the majority of them were still standing there as if they expected something more would follow. Mr. W. was wiping the sweat from his brow while he was speaking with the Japanese man who attends him; in the same time, the other young man began to play on the organ – he had on a simple garment and simple Japanese trousers. He was a little pale, and bending his head and half closing his eyes began to sing this song, 'Jehovah is my Shepherd'. His voice was not high, but he sang nicely, as we hear the showers falling on the olive tree in the Palace of Olympias. The music soothed us. When the music ceased Mr. Waddell began to make his preparation for the homeward journey. He first put on his overcoat, next he wound round his body a long black cloth in length more than ten feet. What did he use the cloth for is a question. Perhaps it may be a protection from cold, but for whatever purpose it is quite curious. His body is increased in roundness by this winding round of the cloth till it became like to a drum. He then putting the Bible under his arm and saluting his companion started away. I was looking after him to see which way he would go. He passing the right side of the oak tree went his way in the middle of the path, went towards the 'Hiro-Kogi'.* The two men who were with Mr. W. cleared the place, and carried the organ by jinricksha. The wind was blowing and fallen leaves were whirling. The dust was flying in clouds.

By Mr. Sakamoto.

The author was clearly, from the classical references, a person of some learning. The preacher's use of parent–child relations to illustrate the

* Hirokōji, the main street in Ueno, still exists.

sermon perhaps owes something to his study of the influence of Confucianism, in which filial obligation features strongly. We note, too, the preacher's use of contemporary events when he refers to the recent war with China. It is clear that he held the listeners' attention.

Ueno (as it is now spelt) lies in what was then the north-east corner of Tokyo, a few miles from the Waddells' home. Hugh's elder daughter Margaret provides her own enchanting, and in some ways complementary, account of a visit to the park with her younger sister Helen to hear their father preach. This was near the end of their stay, when Margaret was about sixteen, and her younger brothers had already left Japan. The entry is dated 'Sunday May 6. 1900', and as usual Margaret records what she read and what she ate:

> *Beautiful* day. Ther. 66°. Began Clifford castle. Dinner of curry & rice. Tates. At 2 went in rickys to park. Papa preached. Many came and listened attentively. No disturbance at all. Several times they smiled. Instead of listening, for some time H & I wandered about. We went up to see the great bronze figure of Buddha, reached by twenty stone steps. Before him, was a great wooden money-chest, a box for sticking incense sticks into, and several flowers. He is sitting, hands joined, knees bent. Enormous height, and hollow. Opposite him on another hill was a huge bell, which was rung by a man, who banged it at intervals with a huge beam. This resulted in a deep solemn mournful musical sound. Coming down from this, we descended 30 steps to visit a fox temple. It was rather small, but had little pillars for itself. The outer room, for it consisted of only two, was shut off from the inner by a lattice door. Here was placed a table with several little painted images representing foxes. On either side of the table was a large yellow fox image. The room was hung all over with lanterns great and small. On the walls were displayed cases (open) containing arrows, some small, some large. Just in front of the entrance door, stood a large money-box. We saw a man worshipping the fox. He knelt on a matting, between money-box and table, bowed his head, clapped his hands, many times. At last took a dark box from the table, shook out, turned it upside down, took out a long thin piece of wood, which he seemed to read. Did this three times (?) then bowed, and left the building. The real fox lived, not in the temple, but in a hole not far from it, approached by several 'torii'* and a paved walk. A little

* *Torii*, the sacred gateway at the entrance to a Shinto shrine. Two upright pillars support a horizontal lintel, upward-curving at its ends, with a straight crosspiece just below. Since the Japanese attitude to religion is non-exclusive, this can also sometimes be found at the entrance to a Buddhist temple.

Torii.

> money-box was hung up before the hole. The man dropping a cent or two into the hole sat with bent knees before the hole, prayed, clapped his hands bowed and withdrew. We now retraced our steps to the service and remained there for the rest of the time. We left at 5 (?) for home. Had long drive of four miles. Had tea. Read. Bed.

That Helen and her older sister were allowed to wander by their broad-minded father is one of the notable features of this description, while another is their great interest in the sites of worship of religions other than their own. The Great Buddha in Ueno Park was a well-known sight, made of bronze and erected in the seventeenth century to rival such statues elsewhere in Japan, though it was evidently a good deal less attractive than some of them and its destruction in the air-raids of 1945 has not been much lamented. The 'fox temple' is not, in fact, a temple but a shrine to the Shinto deity Inari, protector of the local people and also the god of harvests and commerce, whose messengers are the two foxes guarding the entrance to his shrine. The man praying there is clearly trying to read his fortune and invoking the god's assistance in discovering a good one. The diary entry is accompanied by a small drawing of the shrine, with its lattice door and curved roof and a row of little *torii* that can still be found in the park today.

Margaret's diary is written in a thick jotter and runs to about 200 pages. Her father had given the jotter to her, as she records on the cover, where she also writes her age, the date and time that she received it, and her address.[21] The address that she gives is in present day Roppongi, and from Margaret's account we can learn a good deal about the family's life in

A plan of the house, from Margaret's diary.

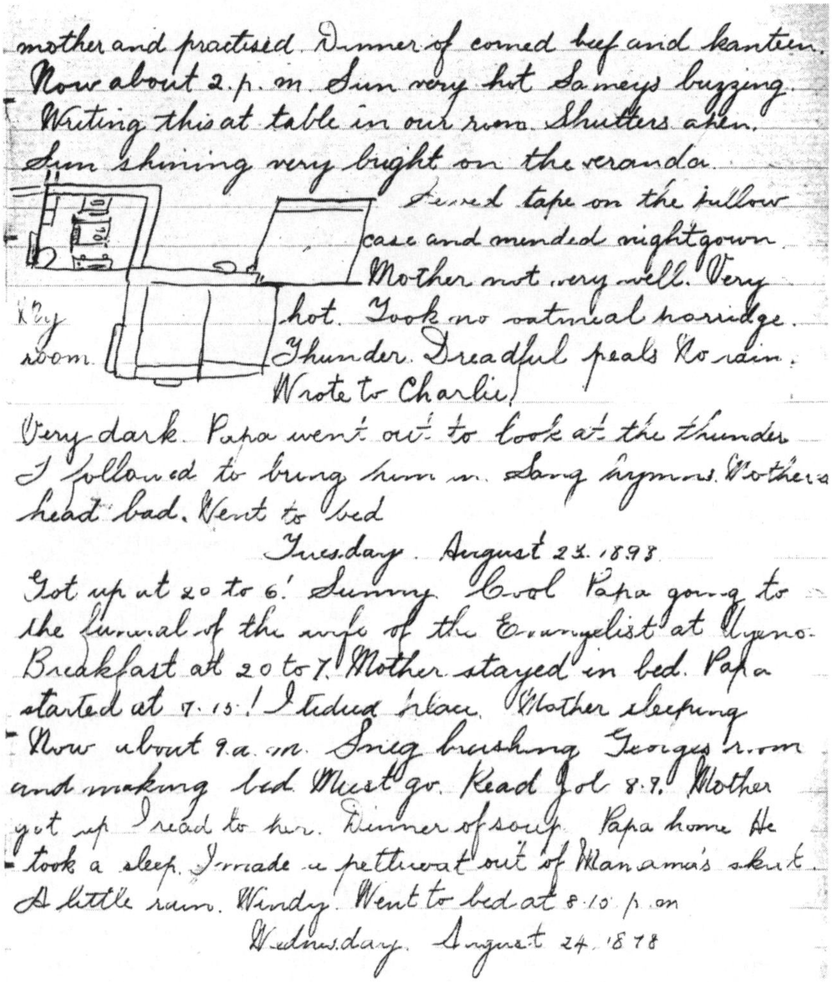

mother and practised. Dinner of corned beef and kanten.
Now about 2 p.m. Sun very hot Sameys buzzing.
Writing this at table in our room. Shutters open.
Sun shining very bright on the veranda.
Sewed tape on the pillow
case and mended nightgown.
Mother not very well. Very
hot. Took no oatmeal porridge.
Thunder. Dreadful peals No rain.
Wrote to Charlie.
Very dark. Papa went out to look at the thunder
I followed to bring him in. Sang hymns. Mother's
head bad. Went to bed
Tuesday. August 23. 1898
Got up at 20 to 6. Sunny. Cool Papa going to
the funeral of the wife of the Evangelist at Ueno.
Breakfast at 20 to 7. Mother stayed in bed. Papa
started at 7.15. I tidied place. Mother sleeping
Now about 9 a.m. Snig brushing George's room
and making bed. Must go. Read Job 8.9. Mother
got up I read to her. Dinner of soup Papa home He
took a sleep. I made a petticoat out of Mamma's skirt.
A little rain. Windy. Went to bed at 8.10 p.m.
Wednesday. August 24. 1878

Tokyo. The diary begins in January 1898 and continues until the middle of 1900, but contains some entries for 1897 which were presumably copied from another notebook or loose sheets and were perhaps the reason that Margaret received the jotter. We know from her descriptions, and even occasionally a drawing, that the house was Japanese-style, with tatami-mat flooring, had two storeys, and was irregularly-shaped, with three parts touching at the corners. The rooms would have been divided from each other by sliding screens covered with thick paper, and from the outside by screens of translucent paper that admitted light, and beyond these sliding wooden doors that would have been closed at night-time or to keep out cold. Although glass windows were relatively rare, it is possible that they may have had one or two, and added curtains, but it is unlikely that the whole house would have been glazed.

The kitchen may still have been earthen-floored and warmth would have been provided by burning charcoal in braziers to heat the rooms, and possibly wood to heat the bath. The bath itself would have been a deep one, the kind used for soaking by the Japanese, who wash outside it. As Westerners, the Waddells may well have compromised on these arrangements. The children may have slept on futons, like the Japanese themselves, though it seems likely that their parents had a bed.[22] We may take it that some of the other furnishings were Western, since items such as a 'sofa' and an 'oven', which are not native to Japan, are mentioned in Margaret's diary.

The garden around the house would not typically have had a lawn, but trees, shrubs and other plants, asymmetrically arranged. The garden seems to have been quite large and the plants various and plentiful. The trees would have been the dominant feature, and we know that these included both evergreen and deciduous varieties, such as persimmon and fir. But what Margaret mentions most regularly are the flowers (plum and cherry blossoms, fuchsia, cowslips, daffodils, primroses, roses, daphne), as well as the fruits and vegetables they grew (strawberries, pumpkins, corn, radishes, melons and lettuce).[23] The natural changes were clearly important to her, along with the welfare of her pets (doves, canaries, even silkworms). The Waddells also seem to have kept a pig, which Margaret fed early in the morning. Tokyo, with a vastly smaller population than it has today (one guidebook gives it at 900,000), still had extensive open spaces then. Although growing quickly, the city 'did remarkably well at preserving a sense of the fields and the moods of the seasons', in the words of one historian.[24]

The house that the Waddell family inhabited was busy with visitors and servants. A housekeeper nicknamed 'Sneg' seems to have been in regular attendance on them, and may have actually lived with them. She certainly accompanied them when they went to other places. Rickshaw men were also sometimes present, according to the diary, and other people came occasionally, to take washing or to do the garden. Most of the visitors to the Waddells' home seem, naturally enough, to have been people connected with the church. These included not only other foreign missionaries, but Mr Wada,[25] Hugh's ubiquitous assistant, and native parishioners. The last would have had to be dealt with in Japanese, and often by Margaret, as the eldest, in the absence of her father, since it is unlikely that her stepmother, who went to Japan only in middle age, could speak the language. The children would have picked it up quite easily, and appear never to have had difficulty communicating with those around them. We

1

2

3

4

5

6

Extracts from Margaret's *kana* workbook. (1) The front of the *kana* reading/writing practice book that belonged to Margaret Waddell. (2) The back of the book, where Margaret wrote her name. (3) Pictures of children studying (Eastern and Western style) at home. (4) Plum blossom/dragonfly/etcetera – images from daily life. (5) A man with bugle, men running to the site of a fire with a pump to put it out. (6) Scholar in his garden.

know that Margaret also studied the written language to some extent.[26] In her diary she records, on 9 January 1900: 'At prayers today I read out of Japanese Bible (to myself!) Papa reads very quick.' Her diary contains a small number of Japanese words, all of them in roman letters.

Among its many fascinating details, Margaret's account does reveal, as her sister Helen's biographer has written,[27] a life of some restrictions and occasional hardship. Besides helping her mother with domestic chores, Margaret undertook an overseeing role for the younger children and also shared her parents' worries about the future. From time to time she expresses concern about her own education too, and the diary is part of her effort to apply herself. The gaps in it, especially in those parts where she intended to record important events outside the family, such as the wedding of the Crown Prince, reveal the difficulties she faced. The style varies between a quick and spontaneous jotting down of things, and passages of well-shaped formal composition. That it was sometimes written late or in a hurry is evident when she says that something happened 'today or the next day'. Yet, despite her many duties, Margaret's life was not without its youthful pleasures, in treats and outings and friendship with other children, both Japanese and foreign. She seems to record everything that she has time to with interest and compassion, and her account has considerable charm.

The portion of the diary for 1897 (but copied in later) is entitled 'Life at Kamakura'. It begins on 4 August, and appears to be unfinished. Kamakura lies to the south-west of Tokyo, on the Miura peninsula. It was the capital of Japan in the thirteenth century, but by this time had dwindled to little more than a village. A contemporary guidebook describes it as a 'sea-side village which is a favourite health resort of the Yokohama residents.'[28] One of the earliest train lines had connected Tokyo and Yokohama, and this was extended to Kamakura in 1890. Sea-bathing as a healthful activity had been largely introduced to the Japanese by foreign residents, and for city-dwellers this was a convenient location. Importantly, however, Kamakura also contained a number of ancient shrines and temples. Its most famous sight was the bronze statue of the Great Buddha about which Kipling had written a now well-known poem following his visit there in 1892.[29] The Waddells, like the other foreigners, went there to escape the heat, though Hugh Waddell continued his evangelising work. Missionaries in Kamakura must have been keenly aware of its profound religious associations, particularly with the Nichiren sect of Buddhism.

The other place to which foreigners withdrew in summer was Karuizawa, which lies on a mountainous plain north-west of Tokyo in what is now Nagano Prefecture. Karuizawa, in fact, started as a place of cool retreat for the foreign population, modelled on the hill stations of

India and elsewhere, and only later became a popular resort for Japanese. Like others among their more fortunate contemporaries, the Waddells took a house there. Margaret's diary records two visits, in 1898 and 1899, and on both occasions these sections have been written in red ink. Though church activity obviously continued, even Hugh Waddell seems to have given some of the time in Karuizawa to rest and recreation. There were many walks that could be taken by the children, their parents and their friends. That Margaret specially added an account of a holiday in Kamakura, and wrote about the trips to Karuizawa in a different coloured ink, suggests that these visits stood out for her. Despite such welcome interludes, however, the family's difficulties were increasing. Church membership had substantially decreased by this time, and Hugh was finding it hard to persuade the Scottish church to continue supporting his work. His worries become evident even in his daughter's diary. In 1899 it was decided by the family that the two boys, Willie (later known as Billy) and George, should return to Ireland and enter school there, which they duly did. Margaret says she misses them, but her younger sister Helen seems robust and cheerful still. In 1900, with his own health failing, Hugh finally left Japan to return to Ireland with his wife and daughters. With his departure, the Scottish Presbyterian Church closed down its mission to Japan. Hugh died in Ireland on 20 June 1901.

Helen Waddell described her father later, in an unpublished autobiographical essay, as 'the Vicar of Wakefield turned Chinese scholar'. Although Hugh Waddell may have died feeling that his life's work was incomplete, the Chinese scholarship that had so long absorbed him was invoked by his daughter in her first published book. Indeed, Helen drew for this upon the library that her father had bequeathed and the volume that resulted, *Lyrics from the Chinese* (1913),[30] was dedicated to him. The story of her happening upon a volume of literal translations from Chinese by James Legge, one day at home when she was deep in other study, and of the enchanting selection of rewritten poems that resulted, has already been recounted elsewhere.[31] It was to her older sister that she wrote in her excitement. Yet there is another letter, undated, but that can be easily dated from its contents, in which Helen tells her sister that she has begun writing stories about Japan.[32] Halfway through a letter on 11 July 1912, Waddell says: 'And I am to get that Jap thing typed – and if possible write one or two more things.' She then talks of an introduction to a literary magazine through Professor Gregory Smith (1865–1932), her Scottish friend and supervisor at Queen's,[33] before reverting to the subject of the stories: 'I have written another – by name "White Iris", which beats the first one hollow – but it's maybe on the principle of the new baby.' Having taken a BA at Queen's in 1911, Waddell had completed an MA the following year and had been accepted for further study at Oxford. But she had declined the opportunity to go to Oxford in order to stay in Belfast and look after her ageing stepmother. It is clear that, in addition to her plans for research, the young scholar Helen Waddell had literary ambitions, and that she was turning to Japan for subject.

It is likely that 'After Strange Gods' was the first story to be written, quickly followed by an early draft of 'The White Iris', both of which are set in Karuizawa. The typescript of the former has been corrected and signed by Helen Waddell, though without a date. It is a first-person narrative, in which many of the circumstantial details can be confirmed from Margaret's diary and other sources. 'The White Iris', in which likewise the setting is quite realistic, is by contrast a third-person narrative and it is almost certain that the existing typescript version of it was completed later. Waddell continued to work on this story throughout the decade, and it is the one most frequently referred to in her letters. Both stories feature only Helen and her brother Billy, who was the next but one above her in age, rather than her brother George, who was the closest. Both also suggest quite a strong identification with the country and its people, though the Japanese words and names employed are occasionally incorrect. Plainly the adult author only half-remembered the language she had spoken as a child. She describes herself and her brother as 'Japs born and bred', in contrast to the other unaccustomed foreigners, in 'After Strange Gods', while in 'The White Iris' it is sympathy for the poor Japanese of their acquaintance that prompts the children's actions. It is notable too that the missionary children are highly receptive to the mystery of a disused Shinto shrine in the first story, and the solemnity of a Buddhist funeral in the second. Their own religion does not seem to preclude or interfere with this. They also respond keenly to their natural surroundings.

There is one further tale in which Billy features with his sister, and this is 'Kwannon of the Single Grace', set in Kamakura. This story is interesting in several ways. Once again there is an adventure by the children, this time at night during the Bon festival, when, according to Buddhist beliefs, the spirits of the dead return, and the children seem highly responsive to the eerie atmosphere along the seashore. Once more, many of the circumstantial details can be confirmed, but the length and route of the children's night-time walk is somewhat unrealistic, showing that the central action has been invented, or at least that the author has adjusted or improved her recollections. The evangelist in this story, we know from Margaret's diary, is a Mr Takahashi,[34] and Miss Van Bilt is the real Miss Youngman, leader of the Ueno Mission, with whom Hugh Waddell sometimes did not get on.[35] The garrulous old woman, and her son the hapless Shinzo, whose story forms the secondary action, add much in range and depth. Whether or not

Miss Kate Youngman.

they are inventions, both of them are quite convincing characters. The dialogue has a natural feel to it and the way that it is represented, especially in the use of negatives ('Is it not a true word, Sensei?' 'It is not a true word.'), suggests that Helen Waddell could recall this kind of conversation in her head. The pilgrim Shinzo's enquiries of the Christian minister also offer a wonderfully believable example of the kind of exchanges that ordinarily took place between missionaries and native Japanese. Notably, too, this story is the only one in which there is any allusion to there being other children in the family, in the reference to other sons. Helen's older sister Margaret is never mentioned in them, and there are only two passing references to their stepmother Martha.[36] Undoubtedly the narrow focus makes the subject matter clearer and easier to handle.

There are two other autobiographical accounts, really more episodes than stories, entitled 'The Keeper of the Door' and 'In Things Evil'. These form one manuscript, and the second, which continues from the first after a space, is unfinished. These handwritten pages appear to be the beginning of an autobiography, in which Billy does not feature. The first part was later typed and appeared as a back page article in the *Manchester Guardian* on 19 July 1915. We do not know exactly when it was written, but it seems probable that it had been drafted somewhat earlier than this. 'The Door-keeper of the Buddha', the title under which it was printed, describes a toad in the garden of the Waddells' house in Tokyo and ends by invoking the Great Buddha in Kamakura for comparison. There is an affectionate portrait of Helen's father and a bemused one of a Church of England clergyman. The girl who appears in the unfinished fragment is the same Kate who appears in 'After Strange Gods', and in Margaret's diary as Helen's closest friend. Probably they attended school together. Her real name was not Lascelles but Large, and she was not American, as Waddell makes her in that early story, but Canadian. Kate lived alone with her mother because her father had been murdered.[37]

That Helen chose to put only herself and Billy into the stories she wrote about her childhood, and no other members of the family except her father, seems puzzling at first. Although Margaret was excluded, we know that she was soon told about the writing of them, as she was again about the Chinese lyrics a little later, and that she remained her younger sister's confidante. The Waddell sisters' devotion to each other throughout their lives is well attested. The mystery is rather that Helen chose Billy, who was the next but one above her and four years older, instead of George, who was closest to her in age and only two years older, as her companion in the stories. Undoubtedly this had something to do with a difference in character or personality between the youngest boys. In the two family portraits that appear in the Corrigan biography, one of the ten children with their father and natural mother, the other showing the children with their father and stepmother, Billy is the only one who is smiling in both pictures. It is an irrepressible, slightly mischievous smile. In the revised version of 'The White Iris', Helen even makes herself and Billy twins.

There is an early passage in Margaret's diary which suggests the individual characters of the children. She records, on 3 March 1898: 'Did a few sums. Now about 6-15 p.m.! George learning history. Helen writing Coral Island about what they did on Monday. Willie did nothing.' Margaret herself, periodically worried about her studies, has made an effort to study, and now falls back on her diary. George is studying seriously, while Helen is engaged on something more creative (a story with some resemblance to R.M. Ballantyne's novel *Coral Island* presumably). Even as a child of eight, Helen appears to have the beginnings of a literary or imaginative gift. It is notable that both the girls are writing diaries, while the boys are expected to study history. We know from a later portion of the entry that this is what Willie, as he was known then, was supposed to do as well as George: 'Papa came home about 7 p.m. Willie's History (not learnt). Played papa waltz. Went to bed at 8 p.m.!'[38] Here Margaret shows us Willie the refractory student, a vivacious boy who cannot settle to his studies. Later, during a trip to Karuizawa, she notes at the end of one entry, on 24 June: 'Now about 7 p.m. Willie reading German Book to Helen & George.' Whether this was a book in German, or a translation from it, we do not know, but it seems a happy scene. On 12 July, however, Margaret more ominously records: 'Pow wow at dinner between Willie and us all.'

Billy Waddell, in a family portrait.

This suggests some argument or conflict, with Willie being called to order by the family. By the next month they are all back in Tokyo, and Margaret writes, on 15 August: 'Willie giving Dove's water. Now about 2.30. Helen and George Painting and Singing…' The next week, on 21 August, Willie is in trouble once again, in a way that George never seems to be: 'Awfully Hot. Rash came on my face. Willie said unkind thing and I cried. Papa went to Uyeno. It is called Nettle-rash…' Other entries see the boys taking walks together and continue uneventfully until the time comes for them to leave for Ireland. But there is a noticeable absence, in Margaret's account, of instances of Helen and Willie spending time or doing things together.[39]

The vitality and waywardness of Willie Waddell that has its first hints in the brief records in his sister's diary, continued into his adult life. When the two boys arrived in Ireland, they stayed with relatives in County Down until they were sent to school. The records of Campbell College, Belfast, show that they were registered as students there in January 1900. We know that they boarded at the school and may take it that they entered the same class or academic year, though there was a two-year difference in their ages. The records show further that William left in July 1903, from the Lower Sixth, without matriculating, while George stayed another year, matriculating in July 1904.[40] Billy may have felt out of place among students who were, like his brother George, younger than himself, though his premature departure does not seem to have adversely affected the progress of his education. He enrolled as a medical student with the Scottish Examining Board in January 1904, perhaps having studied for matriculation privately. He received most of his instruction at Queen's College (as the university was at that time known) in Belfast and in local hospitals. It was a five-year course from which he emerged qualified as a doctor in January 1909.[41] George meanwhile enrolled at Queen's, and took a BA there in 1908. By the time that Helen took her BA three years later, the name of the institution had reverted to Queen's University, as it had been when her father went there. Margaret, after some general studies at Queen's,[42] married the Revd John Dunwoodie Martin, a Presbyterian minister some thirty years her senior, moved to his parish in County Down and received no further education.

It is not easy to establish precisely what employment Billy obtained on completion of his studies, but we know that he later worked as a ship's doctor. Either during his medical training, or more probably some time after, he became addicted to the use of morphine and was treated in hospital for this. His problems are mentioned in Helen's letters to her sister at the time, though only a few of them survive. It was not her habit to date her letters to her sister very precisely, and, in what is certainly the most important of these concerning Billy, the first page is missing too. The letter offers sympathy and reassurance to Margaret over the death of a Miss Quirk, then changes tone:

> Bunnie, I've just rambled, and you've had no news at all. I'm sure you've been wondering that I didn't send you the socks and the address for Billy, but dear, he turned up on Saturday morning, could stand the place no longer. Do not worry about him, dear, for any sake, for even Dr. Irwin is content that he has left, and says he is looking splendid, and that the one thing is for him to get into work at once. He was so miserable at Haydock – nothing to do, nothing to think about, nobody to talk to but morphia-maniacs, or regular lunatics, and he says he was just getting morbid.[43] You needn't be afraid of his going back to the drug. I was talking to him by himself for a bit, and he speaks of it with a kind of shudder, and says he is glad, *so* glad, to be cured, to be a man again, and that he would never have left the place only that he was afraid of it, for his will was getting weaker instead of stronger, and he was wild for something to do.
>
> Peg dear, we'll have to pray for him desperately. But I am in great heart about him. He is going back to Glossop in a day or two to be nearer the shipping companies – and he is likewise trying to get a hospital somewhere. But he says he will take the first job that turns up, as long as it isn't a cargo boat with too much spare time on board. He will never face that again. And he has set his face to the Indian Medical, and Dr. Irwin is encouraging him. He and I have a catchword to hearten us and we shout it at each other parting – 'January 1913' – which is the first exam he will try for. He was over seeing Miss Houston at the Nursing Home, and he tells me they are never done talking about you...
>
> I told him how it was you hadn't written him at Xmas – and he smiled his old smile and said he knew all right.

Shortly after this, with more affectionate good wishes, the letter ends. From what it says, Billy seems to have been treated at a hospital in England. That 'January 1913' is indicated as a time of hope, soon to come, puts the writing of the letter near the end of 1912. This was not long after Helen had started writing stories about herself and Billy in Japan.

Another of Helen's letters to her sister, possibly written in 1913 after Billy's discharge from hospital, when he appears to have been living with his brother Tom in England, says: 'Letter from Billy this morning. No job yet, but he's keeping straight... It's a very cheerful letter, poor old boy.' Another short note, dated only 'Thursday', closes with: 'No more news from Billy. I wrote to him again.' Yet another, likewise dated only 'Sunday', passes on the news that 'Billy is with Tom, but that he has got another job for May' and digresses further about the danger of someone from Belfast who had a bad influence on Billy, turning up again and leading him astray. This was evidently written not much later. Thus Helen's concern about her troubled brother remained in the background as she continued reading and discussing research projects with her former professor at Queen's. 'Gregory', as she called him, gave his approval to her versions of the Chinese poems, and helped her to find a publisher for them. This modest success undoubtedly encouraged her. She was also corresponding regularly with Professor George Saintsbury, the literary critic, in what was to become a lifelong epistolary friendship. Margaret was busy with a young family of her own, and George was studying at Assembly College to become a Presbyterian minister, like his father. Helen had dutifully foregone the opportunity to study elsewhere, in some sense to repay her stepmother for the affection she had herself received in childhood, following the death of her natural mother. In the last book she published, the 60-year-old Helen Waddell described the house that she and her stepmother shared, at 19 Cedar Avenue in Belfast, as a 'thin red brick house', in pointed contrast to her sister's more ample residence in County Down.[44] Yet it was in that house in Belfast that the contents of her final volume had all been written, as was everything collected in the present volume.

In the middle of 1914 Helen Waddell was asked to take over the writing of a column in *Daybreak*, the Presbyterian missionary magazine for children. It was a monthly journal, printed in Belfast for distribution overseas, and her first contribution appeared in July. She began, suitably enough in a column that was entitled 'For the Tiny Tots',[45] with a story about a little dog, and the next month talked about Dr Barnardo. The third piece was entitled 'The Hearer of Prayer', and described a temple in Japan, and the curious custom of prayer practised there, according to which a fortune paper was chewed up in the worshipper's mouth and spat towards the statues of the guardian gods. If the paper stuck, then the prayer would be answered, and from this Waddell drew a moral. It is likely that she had observed this practice as a child, since it is mentioned in Margaret's diary.[46] A description of it can also be found in a well-known book by the intrepid British traveller Isabella Bird (1831–1904).[47] After these few experimental pieces, Waddell settled down to retelling Bible stories. The best of these were collected together some thirty years afterwards as *Stories from Holy Writ*, the last book that she completed.

The travel book by Isabella Bird evidently also lay behind an article that Waddell published in the *Manchester Guardian* in August, her first publication in a journal of that kind. It was entitled 'The Spoiled Buddha' and appeared as a back page feature on 26 August 1914. It was one of several

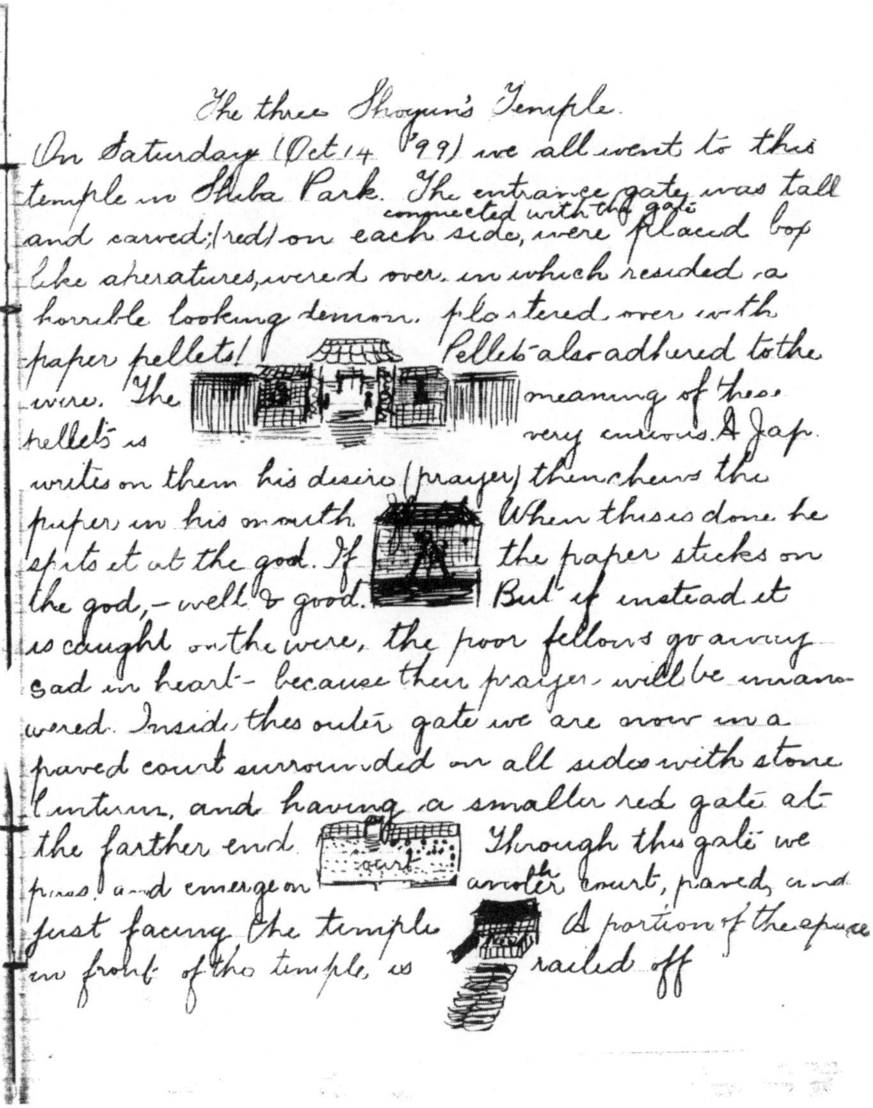

The three Shogun's Temple.

On Saturday (Oct 14 '99) we all went to this temple in Shiba Park. The entrance gate was tall and carved; (red) on each side, connected with the gate were placed box like aheratures, wired over in which resided a horrible looking demon plastered over with paper pellets! Pellets also adhered to the wire. The meaning of these pellets is very curious. A Jap. writes on them his desire (prayer) then chews the paper in his mouth. When this is done he spits it at the god. If the paper sticks on the god, – well & good. But if instead it is caught on the wire, the poor fellows go away sad in heart – because their prayer will be unanswered. Inside this outer gate we are now in a paved court surrounded on all sides with stone lanterns, and having a smaller red gate at the farther end. Through this gate we pass and emerge on another court, paved, and just facing the temple. A portion of the space in front of the temple is railed off

An extract from Margaret's diary describing the prayer customs.

articles she would contribute, but the only one that year. It tells the story of a little-known disciple of the Buddha, Binzuru (originally Pindola), and of how he came to perform the role of medicine god that has been allotted to him in Japan. Binzuru is a minor figure in the Buddhist pantheon, but in the Meiji period there was a well-known statue of him in the temple at Asakusa, on the eastern outskirts of Tokyo. In her book *Unbeaten Tracks in Japan*, an account of a journey that she made to Japan in 1878, Bird describes the temple at Asakusa, which she visited briefly before setting off for remoter parts of the country. She repeatedly uses the word 'popular' in her introductory remarks and comments sharply on the 'buyers and sellers' who crowd the precincts of the temple, invoking Christ's scourging of another temple: 'Not with less righteous wrath would the gentle founder of Buddhism purify the unsanctified courts of Asakusa.' Her wording finds specific echoes in the opening of Waddell's story: 'Binzuru was not *sanctified*; he was only *popular*' (my italics). Indeed, Bird's description of Binzuru accords too closely with the details of Waddell's prose account for it not to have been an important source of inspiration:

> On the right, accessible to all, sits Binzuru, one of Buddha's original sixteen disciples. His face and appearance have been calm and amiable, with something of the dignity of an elderly country gentleman of the reign of George III; but he is now worn and defaced, and has not much more of eyes, nose, and mouth than the Sphinx; and the polished, red lacquer has disappeared from his hands and feet, for Binzuru is a great medicine god, and centuries of sick people have rubbed his face and limbs, and then have rubbed their own. A young woman went up to him, rubbed the back of his neck, and then rubbed her own…[48]

That Waddell was familiar with this book from early in her life we know from her sister's diary. Margaret refers several times to Bird's book in the spring of 1900 and twice mentions it by name. On 31 March she writes: 'Read Miss Bird's Unbeaten Tracks.' A few days later, on 2 April, she says: 'Helen read "Unbeaten tracks" (Miss Bird).' We know that the family had the habit of reading aloud to one another, and that the reading was often done by the Waddell children.

Binzuru was not much remarked as a Buddhist god or figure by foreign commentators, but the statue of him in the Asakusa temple is often mentioned in descriptions of that place.[49] One such record can be found in the diary of Clara Whitney. Three weeks after the Whitney family arrived in Japan in 1875, Clara was taken to Asakusa by a Mr Nakahara, who could speak English. As it happened, the outing took place on Clara's fifteenth birthday, which was 30 August, and was at least in part a birthday treat. Clara and her companion travelled upriver by boat to 'the great temple at Asakusa'. She goes on:

> It is a large structure painted red and is very high. The eaves are turned up at the points which gives it a very heathenish appearance. Many children were running and screaming on the front porch. I remarked to my companion that they did not appear very religious. The interior was a large room filled with many fancy things and idols. Near the door was an idol of wood seated in a squatting position on a pedestal. Mr Nakahara called my attention to the fact that it had neither eyes, nor nose or mouth and it was worn smooth all over. He said it was because it had been rubbed so often by those who were ill. In fact, it was a god of health and any who had a headache could cure themselves by rubbing their hands on the idol's head and then applying them to their own heads, and so on if any other part was affected.[50]

Some priggish comments about deluded heathens follow, though soon after the young author is admiring the physical beauty of a Japanese young man, and, as we know, she later married one. What is interesting about her account is the way that it gives prominence to the statue, which is obviously of Binzuru, in the eyes of a young girl who appears to have noticed little else about the temple. This leads one to think that Helen Waddell's evocation of Binzuru and the temple at Asakusa had some ground in real experience, and that her reading merely acted as a prompt. It is quite probable that she had visited this temple as a child.

It is not possible to be completely certain that Helen Waddell wrote the story of 'The Spoiled Buddha' first, and then extended it to a play of the same title, though it seems the most likely sequence of events. After the article appeared, all the work on the play must have been carried out by the end of 1914, for it was put on the stage early the next year. *The Spoiled Buddha: A Play in Two Acts* did not appear in print for several years, but this story is distinguished by the fact that it is the only one of the author's works to exist in two completely separate published versions.

The story of Binzuru, even as Waddell relates it first in prose, goes well beyond the descriptive account given by Isabella Bird. For a more specific hint of its origin, we must turn to Basil Hall Chamberlain, who acted as Bird's guide when she visited Asakusa. The 1891 *Handbook for Travellers in Japan* that Chamberlain co-authored with W.B. Mason, contains not only a description of the temple complex, including the statue of Binzuru, but also a detailed note on him in the 'List of Gods and Goddesses' included in the book for reference. This latter states that Binzuru, 'originally one of the sixteen *Rakan*, was expelled from their number for having violated his vow of chastity by remarking upon the beauty of a female.'[51] This is the most concrete indication of the central happening in any of Waddell's likely sources, and shows at least that the version of the story she presents had been in circulation. Yet her evocation of it, like her spelling of the word 'Rakkan', embellishes beyond this outline.

When the story is reworked into a play, it undergoes a further transformation, not only from prose to dialogue and dramatic action, but also in that it apparently absorbs the influence of another text. Some at least of the plot and setting of the play appear to have been drawn from a story by Théophile Gautier (1811–72) called *La Morte amoureuse*. In Gautier's tale a young priest is unexpectedly tempted by the sight of a beautiful woman at his ordination ceremony, with disastrous consequences, just as Binzuru is distracted by a vision of a woman in the first part of the play. *La Morte amoureuse*, to which Waddell more than once refers in her later writing,[52] had been translated into English by Lafcadio Hearn (1850–1904) as *Clarimonde*, though we do not know whether she had read this version, for it is quite likely that she read the tale in French.

Though the source of Waddell's knowledge of Buddhism remains obscure, some details of the Buddhist setting are quite accurate, while others are improbable inventions. It is quite true, for instance, that there were originally sixteen Rakkan, the Buddha's first disciples. It is also true that Binzuru, the wayward one, is believed to have been at first a favourite, who had somehow misused his powers and then been cast out from the circle of the elect.[53] His having become a medicine god, with the power to cure physical ailments, is a belief or practice peculiar to Japan.[54] On the other hand, Daruma, with whom Binzuru shares his spiritual exercises in the play, was not one of the Buddha's original disciples, but lived over a thousand years after him.[55] Furthermore, Kwannon, the figure manifested in the distracting vision of a woman and purported to have caused Binzuru's downfall, was not, in fact, originally a woman but a man.[56] As a figure of worship, he is often represented as a woman in Japan and China to show his compassionate nature, but as a bodhisattva or Buddhist saint, he is actually asexual.[57] Yet in the drama, Kwannon is referred to as a harlot. These salient errors suggest that Waddell's real interest lay, not in Buddhism, but in something else.

As a play, *The Spoiled Buddha* lacks dramatic tension and development, and must have been difficult to produce, especially the second act, where the statues in the temple come to life. The billing, when it was brought to performance in February 1915, described it simply as 'a play of Japan', and the audience probably expected something slightly ridiculous, along the lines of *The Mikado*.[58] The richly oriental Belfast Opera House, where the play was performed, would undoubtedly have strengthened this impression.[59] One historian of Ulster theatre, Sam Hanna Bell, observes that 'the esoteric symbolism [of Waddell's play] seems to have been over the heads of the audience and of the players'. He adds: 'Edith Matthews, who saw the first production at the Opera House, remembers that "the setting was very artistic and beautiful and the costumes were good and the acting was fearfully bad".' Evidently Sam Waddell, one of the author's older brothers, '"brought great dignity to the part of the Buddha"', while another member of the troupe 'upset the critics by playing the part of Binzura [*sic*] with a brogue'.[60] It was plainly not a very successful production, and the play has never been revived, but it is significant in several ways.

On a superficial level it is simply evidence of the author's continuing interest in her childhood background in Japan. The Japanese names of all the characters have been employed throughout, presumably to unify the story, and in the first act the women also play the samisen, a Japanese musical instrument, although the first act takes place in India. (The time lapse between the acts, of almost 2,500 years, must be something of a record in theatrical history.) So the outward trappings of the play are almost entirely Japanese. But the way that Waddell imagines the story shows it to have an interpretive, rather than a homiletic, purpose. The Buddha's 'immense affection' for his wayward disciple is obviously something that the audience is meant to share. It is difficult to avoid concluding that Waddell is here in some sense engaging in a debate over the spiritual well-being of her own brother Billy, the prodigal son and lost sheep of the family. The cover of an exotic setting offers her the chance to do this more objectively.

The remote time and place, that cloud and distance what may be the real subject of the play, also provide, on close examination, further meaning. The location of the second act at the temple in Asakusa places the events not only at the heart of a busy entertainment district, but right beside the licensed brothel quarters of the Yoshiwara.[61] These quarters, as Waddell must have known, were an important field of missionary activity in the 1890s. Though this was not something of which the Irish audience would have been much aware, the setting nonetheless adds poignancy to the question of enslavement to the desires of the flesh. In its broaching of this matter, the conflict between bodily desire and spiritual fulfilment, the play becomes an earnest of Waddell's later writing on the Middle Ages. At the same time, the story of Binzuru, who is given the power to heal the sick in body, cannot but remind us of the author's brother Billy, who was trained to do the same.

If Helen Waddell at this time moved away from writing about the East as she had known it in her childhood, to writing about an imaginary Japan, she also paradoxically renewed her real contact with the East. This happened when she met Dr George Taylor, a Presbyterian missionary to

Helen Waddell in her twenties.

India. Taylor was a third-generation missionary, originally of English stock, who had been born in the west of India in 1855 and had grown up speaking Gujarati. He attended university in Belfast, and trained as a minister there, thus forming a connection with the city. He was visiting Ireland on furlough with his wife in 1914 when he met Helen Waddell. We do not know exactly when this occurred, but it presumably came about because of their mutual involvement with the church, and especially because Helen was now writing for a missionary magazine. Taylor's upcoming furlough was announced at the beginning of May, and he probably arrived around the time that she had begun contributing to *Daybreak*. When he got to know her, he was so impressed that he decided to make her an allowance. The Taylors had no children of their own, and the ageing couple came to look on Helen as a surrogate daughter during their stay in Ireland. There was even a suggestion that she might return to India with them for a visit, though this never happened.[62] At the time Taylor was principal of a college for native pastors, Stevenson College in Ahmedabad, which had been closed during his absence. A farewell gathering for him took place in Belfast on 24 November and we may take it that he returned to India soon after that.[63] Helen's affectionate correspondence with him began upon his return to India, and they exchanged letters weekly until his death.

It was during Taylor's visit to Ireland that the first version of 'The Spoiled Buddha' came out as a newspaper article. Whether Helen Waddell discussed it with the man who then became her material benefactor and spiritual mentor, we do not know. She was, however, almost certainly working on the article, and afterwards the play, at the time that her acquaintance with him was deepening, and he may well have been aware somehow of her submerged concern with her wayward brother. Billy, in some sense the hidden subject of the play that she was drafting, seemed meanwhile to have overcome his drug addiction and had gone back to sea. Just before he boarded another ship as surgeon in the autumn, he visited his sister Helen, who wrote of this to Margaret:

> He has got the boat he wrote to J.D. about, and starts on Tuesday away to Rangoon (locality vague?). But he's to be away two months and is cherishing designs on some Indian colonel's – 'elderly ugly daughter' – He was wanting to see you before he went, but was a little nervous about the arrival, so I sent him word that the coast was clear…

This suggests that Billy was held in disgrace, having to visit his older sister secretly, perhaps to avoid the disapproval of her husband, the 'J.D.' of the letter. The ship, a merchant vessel named the S.S. *Derbyshire*, departed from Liverpool on 1 October.

Billy Waddell died in a drowning accident at sea on 21 November 1914, when the ship on which he was serving was returning to Liverpool from Rangoon. He was 29 years old. When the accident occurred the ship was in the Arabian Sea. According to the logbook, Billy was sitting on the taffrail, at the back of the ship, at about 10 a.m., and suddenly fell backwards into the sea, hitting his head as he did so. Someone standing nearby threw a chair overboard, for him to cling to, and raised the alarm, after which lifebuoys with flares were also thrown. Two emergency boats were lowered, and rowed around for an hour, but when no sign of the surgeon could be found, they were taken on board again and the ship went on its way. The surgeon's cabin was then sealed, in accordance with the usual procedure, until it could be examined and its contents listed.

There is nothing in the logbook account of Billy's death to indicate bad weather, and the circumstances in which the accident occurred are certainly mysterious. But 'drowning' is given as the cause of death in the official return of deaths at sea for that year, and the logbook is the only factual record. The listing of the contents of Billy's cabin, made two days after he fallen overboard, shows a relative dearth of personal effects – many clothes but no books except the Bible and Prayer Book, and only one letter, addressed to a nurse in India. There were also four photographs, but of whom we do not know. The logbook adds: 'A few notes have been found in the surgeon's room, but nothing which will lead to his actual home address.'[64] In the absence of this information, there must have been some delay in letting the family know.

The ship which Billy had been sailing on reached Liverpool on Christmas Day 1914, so it is quite likely that his family were not informed about his death until early in the New Year. About the same time, Taylor would have arrived back in India and his correspondence with Helen Waddell would have just begun. Yet there is nothing in her letters that reveals when she received the news of Billy's death or her first reaction to this news. Nor is there anything in surviving correspondence to show how Helen felt about the performance of *The Spoiled Buddha*, her first work to reach the stage, and which was apparently concerned with Billy. The play was presented in Belfast for a week from 1 February.

Helen Waddell's next appearance in the *Manchester Guardian* was made with 'The Flowing Invocation', which came out as a back page article on 3 March 1915. Like its predecessor, it is an invented tale with a setting in a Japan of the present or the recent past. Like its predecessor too, it seems to owe something to the travel book by Isabella Bird, which contains an illustration of the 'flowing invocation' (*nagashi kigan*) of the title, and an explanation of its use and meaning that is close to Waddell's story. 'I have seldom seen anything more plaintively affecting', wrote Bird when she came across it in the 1860s.[65] At that time it was an unusual sight, and today it is a completely unknown one. The story tells, essentially, of a man whose wife has died in childbirth and of his efforts to ease her passage through the Lake of Blood, a kind of Buddhist purgatory. Some of the details overlap with other stories: as in 'Kwannon of the Single Grace', there is a garrulous old woman who rebukes her son for his failure to produce an heir; as in *The Spoiled Buddha*, there are allusions to the sinfulness of Kwannon. But death is a new subject for Waddell in 'The Flowing Invocation', attended as it is by a concern about what might follow death, the fate of the eternal soul. It seems possible that the story was written after she had heard about her brother's death and was part of her response. As in the play, she tries to find some way to exculpate the erring male protagonist.

On 14 April 1915, not long after her correspondence with Taylor had begun, she wrote to tell him about her research, and how she works at it

> in a crescendo of violence until the last paragraph finds me feverish and exceedingly inkstained. Then for a month I go out like the cows to

> grass. The last time it has been several months – but there was a play in between.

Only passing reference is made to the play at this early stage, and Waddell's next contribution to the *Manchester Guardian* was on quite another subject. On 19 May she published 'The Egoist', the first of four short essays she eventually wrote about Ballygowan House, the County Down home of her aunt and uncle.[66] This house had been a possession of the Waddell family for almost 200 years, and Helen had spent many holidays there when she was growing up. She describes the house and its surroundings in a luxurious, romantic fashion, and its romance was extended to the East:

> Its affinities with the East are astonishing. Not the East spiritually, from within, but the gorgeous East, the crude East of the 'Arabian Nights', the East of Begums and rubies which is in old bound volumes of magazines.

This article was followed by another piece about Japan, when 'The Door-keeper of the Buddha' came out in the same newspaper in July.

In spite of the silence about Billy in her letters to Taylor, so that we have no precise knowledge about when the family received the news about him nor how they might have grieved for him, Helen takes Taylor immediately into her confidence when tragedy strikes the family a second time. George Waddell, who had been licensed as a Presbyterian minister on 15 March and had just taken up a calling and preached his first sermon at Donoughmore, in County Down, died suddenly of heart failure on 15 June.[67] He was 27 years old, the nearest in age to Helen, and the second of the four youngest Waddells, the smaller family-within-a-family who had been together in the 1890s in Japan, whom death had taken. Helen wrote to Taylor the next day:

> Don't, dear, be distressed too much. It hurts – but it's not a 'sorrow unto death'. He was so dear that I think Christ looking upon him loved him. And we cared for each other so much that nothing can take him from me.

This was followed a week later by a description of the funeral. Soon after this, on 18 July, responding to Dr Taylor's concern that she might marry hastily or unwisely to compensate her loss and seek protection, she tries to reassure her correspondent. In doing so, she reveals her feelings for this brother closest to her in age, whose death had been so wholly unexpected:

> I saw somewhere – it was quite an indifferent novel – a discussion between two women, both single: and one says defiantly that a single woman has many a time more happiness. 'Happiness?' says the other, 'What does a woman want with happiness? It's things and people to care for.' It came home to me those days just after George died. He had left me so empty; and it was the first time I realised that I someday wanted to marry. And I wanted to have sons of my own. For Peggy [her sister] cared for George in the same mothering way as I did, but she had her wee sons left. He was one of them – but he was all the boy I had, and he came to me about everything, more than to her even. I have got over it now, that sort of hungry wistful feeling, so don't be afraid, dear heart, that I'll be falling in love with somebody just because he needs it very badly. And the wee sons at Kilmacrew [her sister's house] are beginning to get into George's place…

Later that year, she went away for a holiday with her friend the historian Maude Clarke (1892–1935) and they composed a novel together, which afforded Helen some distraction from this grief. The novel, *Discipline*, exists in manuscript but was never published.

Six months later, on 25 January 1916, Helen wrote to Taylor about a dream she had had, involving George and her older sister, and makes perfectly clear the bonds of affection that united them:

> I dreamt about George two nights ago: the first time I dreamt of him since he died. I thought how Peggy and he and I were together; Peggy and I were staying in that old country house I have written you about, and he had come over to see us, the way he used to do, the same old Geo. [pronounced 'Joe'] in his old gray suit, and we were going round the fields together. And yet I knew that he had died. It was one of the perfect times when three are company…

The letter continues with a description of their exchanges, and this section of it ends: 'He has been very near these last days.' The process of grieving, which begins in disbelief, is now moving into acceptance.

A few months later, on 30 May, when she writes of George again, she at last confides to Taylor the truth about the older brother Billy. It comes out almost in a rush, after she has expressed concern about Taylor's health, and reported on her reading about angels:

> *One* I have always seen – George. 'It was impossible that he should be holden.' And I have sometimes wondered if he isn't in quest of that older brother – the Billy of 'White Iris' – 'until he find him'. For Billy

> – I never told you before, for I did not want to distress you, when it was near, had lost his way. I wonder if you ever read Stevenson's 'Old Mortality' – the last paragraphs on his friend who 'somewhere on the high seas of life, with his health, his hopes, his patrimony and his self-respect, miserably went down'. It was drink in that case: with Billy, drugs. And he died fighting, but it was a hard fight. 'Derelict' – he once described himself, with his funny twisted smile – 'Dangerous to shipping'. It was so hard a fight that when the end came so easily and the sea took him, we felt that God had been merciful. George and he were together always when they were little. Billy was not more than six months dead when George went to find him.
>
> I was just twenty-two when I first found out about Billy. After that his death was easy. But of them all, he was the most – loveable is hardly the word, for George was that – and yet loveable *is* the word, for there was always a sort of half-whimsical tragedy about his gaiety, and Geo.'s was too spontaneous for that. He had an ugly mouth – and when he smiled it took the dearest curve I know.
>
> I did not mean to tell you. But you will see why those books you asked me to get – those earlier books with their promise of 'some better thing' even for people like Billy – meant more to me than you know. I don't know why I say 'even like Billy', for he was maybe nearer God than people who justify themselves – or the people who have been fenced – like me – and sin un-noticeably.

It is plain that her preoccupation with Billy, her moral and spiritual concern with his waywardness, had gone on for some time before she wrote this. It is also apparent that she had found out about his drug addiction just before she started writing the stories in which he features, and so it is not unreasonable to interpret these as part of her response.

Very shortly after this, Waddell received an invitation from Edward Arnold, the educational publisher, to retell some fairy stories for children. On 11 July she wrote to Taylor:

> I wrote to him on Saturday, accepting, and since then I have been hard at work on the loveliest of the Japanese fairy tales – I sometimes think of all fairy tales – the story of 'The Princess Splendour'. It is a curious thing about Japanese fairy tales: they do not concern themselves with the happy ending. This story ends with the Princess Splendour restored to her home in the moon, and the Emperor, her hopeless lover, ending his days in grief and faithfulness; but it is a far more delicate thing than any 'and so they lived happily ever after'… It is almost a fairy-cycle in itself, for each of her five suitors has his own story, and so far I have

> only got the length of the third. But it is such exquisite work it's like what Peggy and I once agreed must be the world of the sweet pea: with air like liquid crystal, and all the colours faint and clear.

It was this tale that became the title-story of the posthumous collection of children's stories by her. It is quite a well-known tale in Japan, though of obscure and ancient origin, called *Kaguya-hime* in Japanese, but more often referred to as *Taketori-monogatari* (The Bamboo-Cutter's Tale). It tells of an extraterrestrial princess, who is found and raised by a bamboo-cutter and who turns down all her earthly suitors before returning to her home on the moon. Corrigan takes this tale as a motif in her biography, invoking it as a poetic parallel for Waddell's unmarried life.

Eileen Colwell, who edited Waddell's book of stories, notes the original on which her retelling had been based.[68] This was a translation by an American missionary, E. Rothesay Miller, which had first appeared in the year of Waddell's birth.[69] It was a soft-cover volume, bound with string in the Japanese manner (but on the left to accommodate the roman script), and with many colour illustrations. Among the notably enlivened passages in Waddell's telling, are several resonant conversations between the Princess Splendour and her adoptive father. Waddell introduces reference to the 'Even Pass of Yomi [which] is the entrance to the Land of the Dead', and gives particular attention to the youngest suitor, who loses his life trying to fulfil the Princess's wishes. The Emperor, to whom she explains that 'marriage is not for we fairy-folk', is the last suitor she rejects.[70]

Among the tales that Waddell retold, it is the Oriental ones that seem to be the most elaborate and longest, and which eventually included tales with settings in Arabia and Moorish Spain, but she also worked on other tales about Japan. One of these, 'His Augustness the Prince Fire-Fade', which appears in the posthumous collection, is drawn apparently from Basil Hall Chamberlain's 1882 translation of *The 'Kojiki', or Records of Ancient Matters*, Japan's earliest known chronicle. Partly myth and partly fact, this chronicle purports to tell the early history of the country, beginning with the creation of the land itself. We know that Waddell possessed the volume by Chamberlain, though she may have supplemented her use of it with some of the other versions that were available in English.[71] 'His Augustness the Prince Fire-Fade' is a tale of two princes, who exchange the luck that each had with contrary results, and involves one of them in a prolonged relationship with the daughter of the Sea-Deity. The other tale deriving from this source which Waddell worked on at this time, 'Métier de Femme', is reprinted here.

The substance of 'Métier de Femme' is drawn from the central sections of the *Kojiki*, which mainly deal with the military exploits of Yamato Také, who conquered eastern Japan. Waddell is not concerned with the fighting hero, but rather with his wife, and, in order to give the story focus, she provides a viewpoint. This is, naturally, that of Yamato-Také's wife, Princess Oto-Tachibana. In order to create a story, Waddell conflates two separate episodes from the original, which does not form a continuous narrative but consists only of fragmentary highlights. From among these she takes the well-known story of Oto-Tachibana's self-sacrifice, when she throws herself into the ocean to appease the Sea-Deity, calming the sea and allowing her husband and his men to pass across it. The other episode is that of Yamato Také's dalliance with the Princess Miyazu, which actually occurs a little later in the chronicle. Waddell quite convincingly weaves these two sections together to produce a situation in which Oto-Tachibana is neglected for the other woman, before she finally redeems herself by giving up her life. In the *Kojiki* no such connections are made, but the story benefits from such retelling and recasting, and it is typical of Waddell's imaginative use of primary materials. The configuration was not completely new, however, since a similar one appears in a contemporary travel book.[72] The crude sexual details of the original (which Chamberlain himself put into Latin, to protect the delicate Victorian reader) have been removed. The story appeared in 1916 in *The Victorian*, the magazine of Victoria College, Belfast, the girls' school Waddell had attended. In a letter to Taylor of 7 January 1917, she tells him that the two women represent different aspects of womanhood. She asks herself which is the true métier, and concludes that Oto-Tachibana should not have followed her husband on his exploits: 'Myself, I think Oto-Tachibana was wrong, you know: but so divinely wrong that one gives her the glory of martyrdom without a grudge.'

In 1912 Helen Waddell had told her sister Margaret in a letter that Queen's would not allow her to do, in her supervisor's words, 'an imaginative piece of belles lettres'. Though she continued to consider ideas for research, she was restricted by her decision to stay in Belfast with her ageing stepmother. During the 1910s Helen's writing became increasingly literary and creative. Her delight in the imaginative world of the fairy tales that she was rewriting is apparent in her letters. 'The fairy tales proceed gloriously', she tells Taylor on 8 August 1916, as she reaches the end of the first batch. A few weeks later, however, she is taken to task about her research when she meets her old professor. On 19 September she relates this to Taylor: 'Did I tell you that I saw Gregory ten days ago, and was dealt with sternly? I was to do him an article on Lady Mary Wortley Montagu – for the *Manchester Guardian* – and then return to the Research book.' Though no newspaper article ever seems to have appeared, Waddell is immediately entranced by the subject: 'one of the most fascinating women I know and the most delightful letter writer'. The letters of Lady Mary Wortley Montagu

(1689–1762) describe her experiences in Turkey, to which she had accompanied her husband on a diplomatic mission. Her evocation of the East was a key element in forming the eighteenth-century fashion for things oriental. One senses that Waddell has begun to share the exotic adventure, at least in her imagination. In the same letter in which she comments to Taylor on 'Métier de Femme', she says: 'I'm working these days with immense pleasure at my fairy tales: one especially, a legend of Washington Irving's finding about a Saracen prince of Granada.' And again:

> You are to like the first sentence of my Spanish fairy-tale – 'This is a story of the days when the Moors were Kings in Spain.' It has always had a fascination for me – that Moorish civilisation.[73]

But even as the young woman continued delightedly with her work, the joy of discovery was to be clouded once again with grief.

Margaret ('Meta') Fleming, one of Waddell's contemporaries at Victoria College and then at Queen's, had gone out to India as a missionary in 1912. She died on Christmas Day 1916, though, as before, there would have been some delay before this news reached Helen. In a letter to Taylor on 13 February she described the friendship between Meta and herself at Queen's as being 'that she and I were David and Jonathan'. Taylor subsequently wrote a memorial article for a mission journal,[74] and sent this to Helen. By March 1917 she was back at work, and writing on the 24th:

> I have been working steadily at the fairy tales. The big difficulty is over: I have my material. For India – the *Anvar-i Suhaili*, translated by Eastwick, and – fortunately – far beyond copyright: and for Arabia and Persia, the *Arabian Nights*, in Lane's translation. Did I ever sing you the praises of my own *Arabian Nights*, which leaves me cold before the glories of the stately Library Lane? It was bought in Maruya's, I think, in Yokohama: it's huge and fat and bound in homely scarlet, with a curious air of being sun faded and sun burned. The print is small and very black, and the paper is faintly yellow: again the sense of strong suns and much basking in them is suggested. There are no notes; and only Lane's introduction. And for 'crowning mercy' as Saintsbury would say, there is added 'from another source' the perfect version of *Aladdin* and *Ali Baba*. And there are no illustrations. I confess a debt to the abused and miscalled Library Lane, for I have to go to him for distinguishing the sources – Arabian and Persian.

Other stories mentioned come from France and Scotland.

Waddell's *Lyrics from the Chinese* had recently reached its third edition, and the romantic preface to that book – 'It is by candlelight one enters Babylon.' – anticipates in many of its details not only the work she was now doing on the fairy tales, but even some of her later writing on the Middle Ages. The suggestive 'candlelight', by which she herself retired each night, is something of a yardstick for poetic evocation. She picks up on this in writing to Taylor on 3 April:

> I did like your coin paper: it is 'candlelight': coins are to history what lyrics are to literature. Myself, I think the face might very easily be a rather horrible 37: there is youth in it still, though a sinister youth. And I like the 'bypath meadow' to the sun, especially after much reading in the Arabian Nights: do you remember the oath of the wicked Persian in *Hassan of El-basrah*, 'by the fire and the heat and the shade and the light'.
>
> And your exposition of the almond tree has something of candlelight too. There was a plum tree in the garden in Tokio, that came out almost in the snows – a tiny pink plum tree, with black branches. By the way, did I ever send you one of the unpublished 'Lyrics from the Chinese': I kept it back because it was so much later, so sophisticated and self-conscious beside the earlier work – a 'from a College window' A.C. Bensonish performance, but rather pretty in its way.
>
> 'Last night the east wind blew with bitter rain,
> And stripped the wood and strewed the branches far,
> And all the little river boats swept in,
> And wrecked them high above the river bar.
>
> Yet all night long beside my window pane
> This old uncared-for plum tree slept alone,
> And now spreads out its branches, gaunt and grim,
> Clean washed and glittering in the early sun.
>
> A few half-drownèd buds show faintly pink,
> And their small fragrance smote upon my heart,
> A better painter might think scorn of it,
> But their faint laughter is beyond my art.'

Customarily her letters cover several pages, and often take up matters of faith and family concern, but once again she reports on her commission in this missive: 'The fairy tales go on famously. I am doing Gaelic ones just now; they are so fresh and clean and swift after the musk and heavy "oily" scents of Persia.'

An encounter with Gregory Smith in May produces the accusation that

Waddell is failing her gifts by not concentrating on more intellectual work, a truth which she acknowledges to some degree when she reports the incident to Taylor on 7 May. But she adds, in mitigation: 'No man – certainly nobody academic – understands the continuous petty exaction of a house.' Soon after this Waddell's developing imagination returned to China, and began to mine it for material. In a letter to Taylor on 10 July she makes the first mention of an article 'on Chinese literature as the eternal eighteenth century, which has been so long brewing'. She also tells him that she has lent the volume of Legge's translations of Chinese poetry from which she drew her Chinese lyrics, to someone and is longing for its return.

Few of Taylor's letters to Waddell have survived, and most of those that have are only fragments, so that we must rely heavily on her side of the correspondence to reconstruct it. But Taylor was a man of wide interests, ranging from mathematics and theology, to history and literature. While meeting him largely on his own terms intellectually, Waddell more vividly personalises what she says, which occasionally means going off on tangents of recollection. We do not know what comment prompted this memory of childhood on 23 July:

> That Ludwig reminds me of a young German officer on the boat going out to Japan – he was third officer, I think, and a dear. His Christian name was Ludwig, and I've forgotten the other. But I've still fragments of the things he gave us. I don't suppose the boy had much, but he simply emptied his pockets on us four at every port – Turkish delight, and cocoanuts and fans, and he spent all his spare time playing with us. Peggy was almost thirteen then, and I was seven, and the two were in between. We did love that young man, and he wrote to us for years, and was answered in a quadruple letter. Then one of his letters wasn't answered, and we lost his address, and I wonder sometimes what became of him. And what has happened to him now.

An aching sense of loss informs this, besides an awareness of the war. If her memory is correct, then the children's second journey to Japan was made in 1896. But in 'The White Iris' she gives her age as six.

By late August Waddell is reporting difficulties with her writing, as she tells Taylor on the 22nd: 'Do you know I'm writing dreadfully badly. I did half an article on my dear "Chinese eighteenth century": and it is a hopelessly uninspired performance.' The same letter, and the next, mention 'little Mr Santo', a Japanese man studying theology in Scotland, and also in difficulties.[75] Waddell tries to help him, but observes on 28 August, when he has come to visit, that 'the language is such a handicap to me: and it is hard for him to get his problems into intelligible speech'. It is clear that she has lost most of her spoken Japanese. 'I haven't often liked anyone so much', she says, and: 'He says he will keep on writing, and Mother gave him the addresses of some people in Tokio, Mr. Wada for one, the man my father trained and ordained over his own congregation. He was a dear, so far as I remember, very grave and gentle, and a fine head.'

Japan, and those who peopled Waddell's childhood there, have become, like that period of time itself, inaccessible to her. Yet Waddell's strong affections from the past infuse warmth into those of the present. Near the end of the year, on 4 November, still troubled by the article on China, she describes a visitor from Australia:

> I hadn't seen this 'Robert' since I was in short skirts and round spectacles, and himself a long weedy youth taking lectures in Edinburgh. He has filled out tremendously, has a small daughter… and reminded me curiously of Geo. The same funny blend of shyness and mischief and sheer friendliness. We liked each other awfully, and he wrote to me after he got back asking me to let him be a friend of mine. And would I write to him now and then? And let him know about anything I wrote. It was like one of Geo.'s letters. The same self-abusive growl about being such a poor minister and so shy of talking religion to people. And I found myself writing him one of Geo.'s letters.

But three weeks afterwards, writing on the 25th, it is rather Billy who seems to lie behind her remarks on a conversation she has had about Theosophy, the subject of some recent lectures:

> Helen Beatty was discussing it with me. She doesn't believe it, but admits that it seems to solve some things – inequality of birth, inequality of chances, inequality of pain: – that awful awful doctrine of always getting one's deserts. She said too, that it seemed optimistic to her: their thesis that life was a spiral up to God. I wonder how they sustain that thesis. If it is an evolution, what about the people who begin so fair, so near the top, nice boys, with the kingdom of heaven just across the threshold – and end in dust and ashes and disfigurement. I told her what I could not bear was the awful risk: that what one life won, a very little might jeopardise in the next; that it was easier for me to believe in the transfiguring touch of God. Not always in this life, but in that other, when one is free of the flesh.

She also gives her mentor a detailed account of the sale of Ballygowan House, another lost setting of her childhood, memorialised in an article for the *Manchester Guardian* that appeared soon after.

Just a week later, on 2 December, she tells her correspondent: 'I was working at a Chinese article this week and digressed to two Japanese lyrics.' Then she quotes the two short poems included in the final version. She continues, with Billy clearly in her mind:

> By the way, those two lyrics have a sort of poignancy for me that they would hardly have for other people. I sent them in a letter to Billy, telling him that he was sometime to find me a *Kakemono* [hanging picture scroll] with a hidden bay between two headlands, because he and I would be small children in pith helmets, playing there to all eternity. It missed him at one of his ports: and came back to me from the Dead Letter Office. He never got it. And I never see that lyric about the hunter of dragon-flies that I do not remember him. And remember on the heels of it that he may not have gone so very far.

The completed article was published under the title 'The Hyacinth Fields' in the *Nation* on 12 January 1918. This time in her approach to China, Waddell drew not only on Legge, but also on another equally encyclopaedic source, the two volumes of Herbert A. Giles's *Chinese Biographical Dictionary*, which provides vivid descriptive accounts of important figures in Chinese literature and history, from emperors and court officials to poets, provincial governors and military leaders. Her idea of China in the eighteenth century is based on a selective reading of the short biographies, ignoring those of men who were involved in battles for power, in favour of the poets and scholars who withdrew from all this to cultivate their gardens. Gardens are specifically mentioned in the second half of the essay, and the life they represented was one of scholarly and literary pursuit, of peaceful contemplation and creation. There can be no doubt that Waddell's conception of the eighteenth century was greatly influenced by George Saintsbury, her other important correspondent.[76] It is notable that the locus of such a way of living for the Waddell family, Ballygowan House, had been sold not long before.

The main idea expounded in the essay is that of an imaginary and ideal world somewhere out of sight. The first title for the piece – 'The Jade Partition' – deleted on the handwritten version, suggests the sense of separation. But the idea of the 'bend in the river' reworks an idea Waddell had already elucidated to Taylor eighteen months before. She introduces it in acknowledging a book on Indian fairy stories he had sent her, in a letter of 27 June 1916:

> The book is a beautiful thing. One of the pictures I especially love – the twilight one of the green peacocks. I love indefinite things – I think that is why I so much prefer Japanese art to Indian – now you

> aren't to ruffle, for I'm nearly sure you do yourself. The Indian fairy stories are delightful – I can read them for hours, just the way I used to read Grimm's, and I do admire the 'continuous narrative' of some of them. But they haven't all infinity behind them like the Japanese legends. What I love about Japanese art is their trick of leaving you with a folding of the hills that you can't see behind. One of the things I like best in the house is a very cheap Japanese fan – we had dozens of them, for use not ornament – and this one is very dingy.[77] But it has a glimpse of a bay, and then a headland with pines on it, and behind it one knows there is a smaller bay, for the shore juts out again. But you don't know what it is like, and your mind goes round that headland every time. I am half inclined to write something on it. It would be so easy to pretend that Billy and Geo. and I were little again, and playing on the sands the way we used to do at Kamakura. And for that reason one would never try to go round the head – They would be so easily startled.

This was also before she had received the commission to gather and rewrite the fairy stories, and been distracted by them. Now that the essay on poetry has been published, she wonders about the response to it, and writes to Taylor, on 11 February 1918:

> I am curious to know what you will think of *The Hyacinth Fields*. There's divided opinion about it here. Some tell me it's too difficult: far too subtle. But the curious thing is that the two simplest men I know, Professor Symmers and my big brother in the West country, think there is no obscureness in it: it goes to them like running water.

The brother in question is the other writer in the family, Sam.

A couple of months later, on 9 April, Waddell confides to Taylor, in the midst of her domestic duties: 'I'm being haunted with scraps of Japanese verse, from an old book of my father's that I turned up the other day.'[78] She offers several, including the poem quoted at the close of the Corrigan biography. As is her wont, Waddell adjusts the wording slightly when she reproduces them. A week later, on 17 April, she is in much the same frame of mind with another of her brothers, Martin:

> We didn't lunch yesterday – at any rate, it was very belated. For Martin is a gypsy, rather, and when we left the house and the sun shone on us he said 'Let's go to the back of Cave Hill instead', which we did. It's a bare road – through bogland, and when you've walked half an hour you might be in Donegal. It was the thing I needed to make me

absolutely well again: and Martin eyed my complexion after an hour of it and said approvingly: 'You're not the same girl I brought out with me.' I verily believe I was born under a hedge, and when I revert to that estate it's like a fish going to water. We sat on the heather for a while, me being encompassed in Martin's overcoat which he falsely denied any use for: and I told him scraps of Japanese verse, and he told me stories of what he did when he was little in Japan: one delightful tale of visiting a little Japanese house, a solemn unauthorised trio, aged I suppose from seven to ten: and the extraordinary gratification of their hosts. They inspected the foreign children very minutely, being especially intrigued by their hair: and hailed every remark with profound reverence. Jim was a fervent evangelist at that age, and pointing severely to the Buddha on the Butsudan [altar stand], denounced the worship of idols with great fluency. And the dears, instead of being angry, bowed profoundly, and set the Buddha into a cupboard. Now did you ever know finer manners than that?

It is an entirely believable story. And the exercise of memory, with its awareness of a world elsewhere, recalls an extract in Margaret's teenage diary. On 21 August 1898, the day that she had nettle-rash, she reports: 'Papa came home late. We sat on veranda and talked of Cavehill.' We do not know what prompted this conversation, but Cave Hill was not the only place that Margaret was given to recalling. The previous month she had recorded, on 28 July: 'I drew plan of Ballygowan House.'

Meanwhile, Helen has completed her article on 'Lady Mary' and is trying journals with it. Her success with the *Nation* means that she becomes an occasional reviewer, but the more important consequence she reports to Taylor on 18 May:

> You will be pleased by a letter I got this morning: an important affair, headed 'The American Asiatic Association', and signed by a Miss Emerson, assistant editor of *Asia*, which purports to be the journal of the Association. She had seen *The Hyacinth Fields* in the *Nation*, and was writing to ask me to let them have some of my work for their magazine...

After quoting the letter, she considers: 'I'm wondering if by any chance I've found an open field for *After Strange Gods* and *White Iris*. But I'll wait till I see the magazine. It may be too heavy for sketches as childish as those.' More significantly, however, she continues:

> But at the moment the great BOOK is beginning to exert its old spell. I went to see Gregory on Wednesday, and he was in his best listening

> mood. And I told him all the theories that have been growing in me these three years since I last wrote at it: they've finally taken to themselves a body… It's the struggle dating from the Middle Ages, between love and the thing called love, which good old Fielding says is an appetite as gross as any of the others: the damning of all love by the Church, confounding the love which is of the imagination with the love which is of the senses only, in their ideal of virginity.

This outline of her research plans not only looks forward to her later writing on medieval subjects, but clarifies the theme adumbrated in the play. She expands on her ideas for her correspondent, and the letter ends: 'It's *very* good to be alive when your brain is seething like this!'

Presented with the opportunity for publication in America, Waddell quickly abandoned the thought of sending old material and set about writing something new. She reveals the subject of the piece that she is working on in a letter to Taylor that was written probably in June, or at the beginning of July. Only a fragment of it remains:

> I have been working of late at an article for *Asia*, not on Japanese verse, which has to be written 'in an artist's humour', but a sort of dream-article on *The Uttermost Isles*: the Japanese variant of the Orpheus and Eurydice legend, and with it, its descendant after I suppose two thousand years, the story of *The Peony Lantern*: how a *samurai*'s dead love returned to haunt him on the seventh night of the seventh moon,* which is the Feast of the Dead: and brought him to death himself. It is a Buddhist legend, and one sees the fear of love, because it binds a man's soul so close to the illusion that is the world: with the coming of love there comes a darkness, and what was vain and transitory and a passing show stands still, and eternity flows past like a river of stars. And nothing will shake the darkness, or give the man's spirit the eyes of discernment again:
>
> There is no lantern can lighten
> The dusk of the Way of Love.
>
> Japanese verse is for May and April and September, but this silent drowsy month is for its legends. Do you know, sometimes I have great pity for the people who don't write – or rather (for I write dreadfully little) who don't write things in their heads.

---

*In fact the seventh night of the seventh moon is the date of *Tanabata*, or the Star Festival, but the error was corrected in the printed version.

In a letter to India on 7 July she gives some indication of the deeper thought behind what she is writing:

> The article on *The Uttermost Isles* matures slowly. I've been thinking of the most bitter-sweet of all dreams, the restoring of the dead. 'Women received their dead raised to life again, and others were tortured, not accepting deliverance that they might obtain a better resurrection.' I learned all Hebrews by heart when I was little, and I always pondered over that antithesis (for I took it for actual antithesis) thinking how great faith it took to refuse the intimate sweet sureness of return to this world. And I'm thinking how St. Paul fought that absorption with things seen, the craving that it might be possible for flesh and blood to inherit the Kingdom of God. And his way of fighting is to overwhelm flesh and blood with the intolerable glory of the spirit – sublimation by the heat of its fire: 'mortality swallowed up by life'. Over against him the Buddhist in the same warfare; but his weapons are carnal. It is as though they took one sentence of St. Paul's: 'neither doth corruption inherit incorruption'. 'Spirit must brand the flesh that it may live.' [Meredith] You'll see the inwardness of this disjointed paragraph when *The Uttermost Isles* actually reaches you. The root of both legends I'm working at is the depredation of death, its revelation of the 'body of our humiliation'.

The essay, or *récit*, that she eventually submitted to the journal, was completed quickly and is by far the most substantial of her writings on Japan, or indeed of all her work until this time.

The sense of her own abilities that Waddell gained from this task seems to have given her the confidence, at an important moment in her life, to turn down a lucrative offer of employment. In mid-July her name was put forward as a candidate for the position of headmistress of a girls' school, and then the offer came, but after some agonising, she refused it. Writing to Taylor on 21 July, she vividly describes what the job might mean to her, and what she might accomplish through it. 'And on the other side – "The Uttermost Isles"': a touchstone of intellectual endeavour and imaginative engagement. Despite the excitement of the opportunity, when she went once more to the university,

> before I ever crossed the Library threshold into the familiar oak-scented darkness, the wave had ebbed, and an awful weariness had fallen. And I knew I'd come home. The long quiet empty spaces, and the dim shelves row on row down the passages where only the likes of *me* are allowed to go. And little grey withered Mr. Salmon apologising in his husky voice for the incompleteness of their set of Gautier.

Then she knew that she had made the right decision.

A week later, on 28 July, she writes to say that '*The Uttermost Isles* is written at last':

> I have never felt such 'deliverance', as when the last word of *The Uttermost Isles* was written. For though I loved the doing of it, I was oppressed with that dragging sense of impotence more than usual. Fair copying, it seemed very poor stuff: and it's only re-reading it now that I realise how much went into it. Now the long-postponed article on Japanese verse is coming up over the horizon again. I would be well pleased if I had it written by the end of August.

But instead of getting on with the article she proposes, she is taken up with a review, and on 18 August writes:

> I was inordinately pleased last week to get my first book for review. It's really like one's first patient. It was from the *Nation*: Arthur Waley's Chinese poems, just published by Constable…
>
> Now and then the verse is poignant: but for the most part the perfect metaphor is in one of their own poets:
>
> 'The evening river is level and motionless –
> The spring colours just open to their full.
> Suddenly a wave carries the moon away
> And the tidal water comes with its freight of stars.'[79]
>
> There is not much 'moonshine' in their poetry: but – the slow river with its freight of stars.
>
> It has interested me extraordinarily, as a sort of solvent for the article on Japanese poetry. They have nothing of the sudden 'capture' of Japanese verse. Like us, they prepare the way.

As so often in her letters to Taylor, she includes sentences that will later make their way into print, portions of what she is preparing. So it is with her review of Arthur Waley.[80] Her next letter, on 25 August, starts: 'The *Fortnightly* has accepted *Lady Mary*. This should be in red ink and capitals to convey the exhilaration.' Along with the news and comments on religious matters that the letter contains, she also tells her correspondent that she is sending him a manuscript copy of 'The Uttermost Isles', albeit 'dreadfully dishevelled', and then closes mysteriously: 'The thought of the book is still with me, and is like a hidden glow.'

'The Uttermost Isles', which Waddell had now completed and despatched to the editors of *Asia*, begins with the *Arabian Nights*, moves on to consider the Buddhist attitude to death and ends by retelling a story, taken from a book by Lafcadio Hearn, about a man tempted to rejoin his lover in the next world, and eventually yielding. As with the preceding essay, it is replete with other literary references and allusions, although the tale from Hearn takes up almost half of the text. As with 'The Hyacinth Fields' again, it is not simply a wandering fancy, but follows an idea. The subject that it deals with is the separation wrought by death, and the longing then to be reunited.

Waddell draws on the fairy tales that she has been reading when she introduces 'the story of Hasan of El-Basrah', who lost the woman that he loved and was exiled to the Islands of Wak-wak. She mentions a footnote in the edition by E.W. Lane that she had used, 'to the effect that the Islands of Wak-wak are to be identified with Sarawak in Borneo', but omits the part of his note which says that they have also sometimes been thought to represent Japan.[81] Ignoring this widens the geographical and imaginative range of the opening passage, but seems a little disingenuous. Again, although the subject of death and longing for reunion is not unnatural in view of Waddell's own multiple bereavements,[82] there is nonetheless an obscure suggestion, in her indirect approach, that the main subject may even yet be Billy. Almost immediately we find ourselves before 'the Even Pass of Yomi, which is the halting place between the living and the dead', the same place to which the Princess Splendour lost her youngest suitor, the only one who sincerely tried to carry out his task. Some similar, biographically obscure bereavement, seems to lie behind the poem of Heine's that Waddell quotes from twice.[83] The resonances multiply the further we investigate this densely textured piece of writing, which is mainly, but now perhaps only ostensibly, concerned with China and Japan. Some of the references, such as those to Milton, Donne and Shakespeare, obviously derived from Waddell's readings in English literature at Queen's, just as the Chinese and Japanese references were drawn from readings in her father's library. But there is one other important point of entry to the essay, a full interpretation of which would require an essay to itself, and that is the mention of Gautier. We recall that Waddell had been searching for Gautier in the library at Queen's just prior the writing of this piece, and also that she had drawn some of the inspiration for her play from Gautier's story *La Morte amoureuse*. The connection to the play, and beyond that to her troubled brother Billy, suggests a proliferation of allusions deriving from a single source. The writing itself is densely allusive in what was to become Waddell's mature scholarly style.

In his English translation of Gautier, Hearn admires the 'beautiful weirdness' of the Frenchman's tales,[84] and it is a weirdly beautiful tale from one of Hearn's books about Japan that supplies the main part of Waddell's essay. It is, however, only one of two connected tales, the first of these the 'Japanese version' of the Greek legend of Orpheus and Eurydice, which has already been invoked. The story of Izanagi and Izanami, the brother and sister whose union led to the creation of Japan, is taken once more from the *Kojiki*. Waddell's version of the story is greatly simplified (there were many more gods and islands), and, as elsewhere, she has removed the cruder references to childbirth and copulation, those parts which Chamberlain put into Latin.[85] Some of the Japanese quotations come, as she acknowledges, from Hearn's *Gleanings in Buddha-Fields* (1897), but the main story comes from another of his books, *In Ghostly Japan* (1899), where it has the title 'A Passional Karma'. A close analysis of this text confirms Waddell's claim that she has used another source as well, a direct translation from the original novel in Japanese, but this has not yet come to light. Chamberlain is noted as the translator, and the details which Waddell has interpolated, such as the *hokku* (haiku), are found in the original by Enchō,[86] though not in Hearn. Unlike Hearn again, Waddell refers to the male protagonist by his family name, while his lover is called by her given name, the practice Enchō often follows. That the dead woman bears the same name as her counterpart in 'The Flowing Invocation' suggests once more a coincidence of theme and origin.

Notably, Waddell introduces the main story of her essay as 'the Japanese contemporary of *La Morte Amoureuse*': Gautier's tale first appeared in 1836, before Japan was opened to the West. Like 'The Peony-Lantern', it tells of a man who is drawn toward death by his deceased beloved, and she too has a lantern. But Gautier's protagonist is a Catholic priest, and the woman, Clarimonde, is a kind of succubus. Like the man in Waddell's, or rather Enchō's, story, the priest is the victim of possession by an evil spirit, but he survives to tell the tale. Gautier emphasises the indistinguishable division in his personality – between good and evil, dream and reality – making it a Jekyll-and-Hyde story. By contrast, Waddell's setting is 'Tokyo at the end of the eighteenth century with daylight on its streets'.

Despite the speed and excitement with which 'The Uttermost Isles' was written, the sheer range of reference in it suggests that Waddell had been dwelling on this theme for some time. More than that, the references she makes seem to give some indication of her state of mind before she set the essay down. *Troilus and Cressida*, the other text through which Waddell refracts the central story, is certainly one of Shakespeare's more gloomy and disheartening plays. Apart from Pandarus's role as go-between, Waddell refers directly to only one scene, which is the first meeting between the lovers.[87] This is one of the happier moments in the play, but even here Cressida's speeches contain hints of the betrayal that is to come. Gautier's tale, though powerfully evocative and psychologically telling, is yet a morbid and introspective piece of writing, as indeed is the poem by Heine that Waddell quotes in preparation. In making a second reference to Heine, she places her quotation next to 'Donne's *Relique* and *Nocturnal*', and it is perhaps here that we can find some clue to her deeper mental state. If 'The Relique' echoes the same longing for reunion with the dead that the essay as a whole expresses, 'A Nocturnal upon St. Lucy's Day' is a more introspective and perplexing poem. More than simply loss and longing, the latter poem also conveys a sort of scornful and aloof withdrawal. The determined focus of the poem suggests that Waddell may have been suffering not only from protracted grief but also from depression. She certainly had reason to feel despondent at this period of her life, since she had already spent several years looking after her demanding, and by now also alcoholic, stepmother, for whom she had had to sacrifice many of the pleasures of her own life. She was approaching 30 and had as yet had no chance to use her brilliant gifts in their full measure.

But the next month another opportunity presents itself, and she writes to Taylor on 24 September:

> I have done nothing for a week but be lazy, and read, and write not at all – except the letters that come upon one daily. And I'm mightily refreshed. It's such fun to read for one's own pleasure, with no thought of reproduction. And I have a curious exhilaration upon me; partly I suppose because the Talbot Press in Dublin wants to bring out *The Spoiled Buddha* in their Booklet series, and though I'm not sure whether I want them to, it's not unpleasant to see publishers on the horizon again. They are new publishers, and intelligent: I mean they're not so keen on making money as the 'trade' across the water is for the most part. They really care about getting hold of new stuff. My brother, the 'Rutherford Mayne' one, had sent them the MS. though I didn't know it, and their reader writes back that he likes it, and I have only to consent. The terms are that they, unlike my friend Constable's, take full risks. The author gets nothing until 250 copies are sold – after that 10% royalties.
>
> Now I'd close with them at once, only that I rather wanted *The Spoiled Buddha* to come out with the rest in the book that is some day to be, possibly even to give the book its name. For in a curious sort of way it sums up a lot of my thinking in ten at least of my nine and twenty years, the struggle between negation and enrichment. The great drawback is that I do not much like the mélange of play and prose that publication with stuff like *The Uttermost Isles* and the M.G. articles would be. Artistically, and not sentimentally considered, it *should* come out alone. But I hanker after all the eggs in one basket...

The cover of *The Spoiled Buddha.*

Whether this is the book that she mentioned before to Taylor as a 'hidden glow', or whether that one was to draw upon her research, there seems no way of being certain. But clearly she considered making a book of some kind out of her writings on Japan. She consults her nearest adviser, Gregory Smith, about the project, and reports on 29 September: 'Gregory is very determined against including *The Spoiled Buddha* with the "Collected Works"… It is an uncomfortable bed-fellow, a play: as he says, one is not in the humour for continuous prose after it.' With the offer in hand, and approval from those around her, Waddell set about her revision of the play, and since the only surviving version seems to be a typescript of the printed version, we have no way of knowing how this may differ from the play that was performed. Yet it seems likely that her revision would have consisted only of polishing the text.

Despite a temporary autumn illness, Waddell's work went forward. That Helen was not alone in her absorption with memories of childhood, is evident enough when she writes to Taylor on 8 December about her sister Margaret being ill, a victim of the influenza epidemic:

> Did I tell you that Peggy had been up all night with Sydney [her son]… herself with a temperature of 103. 'Another night', she said, 'I knew I was delirious, but it amused the children and kept them quiet, so I said the things out loud. It was a bay I saw, a bay in Japan, with green pines on the headland, and warm yellow sand. It was quiet and sunny, and oh so far off. Why does one never think of Irish coasts – it's the East. And then it was the water under the pier when we were coming into Genoa in the early morning, the lights in the water among the piles.' I listened and vowed that someday when I rise and go, Peggy is coming with me.

The same letter acknowledges a response from him that has unfortunately not survived:

> Ah, but I'm glad you liked *The Uttermost Isles.* I loved your interpretation: and yet, it wasn't mine. Mine was a sadder thing: I thought of that story as the infinitely tragic commentary on the Buddhist thought of death and love. I didn't want to point the moral: but I deliberately flung St. Paul's 'mortality swallowed up of life', blazing against the darkness.

Yet it is difficult retrospectively to think of her engagement with Buddhism as central to her purpose. Whatever her purpose might be, however, it is not to be prescribed. The letter concludes, apparently in self-defence:

> For I cannot bear 'preaching' unless it is of the essence of the thing written. I loathe the didactic purpose … Things are no good artistically, they don't live, if they haven't 'written themselves': and if you're perpetually in the right temper, they'll write themselves 'lovely and of good report' … I do come back with great relief to the Creator's absence of didactic purpose when he grew wild hyacinths in drifts under trees.

A week later, on 'Sunday afternoon, about four o'clock', with her stepmother quietly in bed asleep, Helen comes downstairs to begin her weekly missive to her mentor:

> If half one's spirit abides with one's friends, which is my conviction, there's something of it too in one's things. This old desk of mine seems just to open its heart to me when I sit down before it: and the pile of books on it – I could stroke them for sheer love. I'm no scholar; but after a long interlude like this which has lasted from the beginning of

> November, I come back to them as if I came home. It's a poor return you have from me in the way of 'research' my dear, and my heart smites me many a time for being a fraud. Surely by the New Year I'll get something done.

The second half of the letter, composed upstairs at ten o'clock that evening, opens with a paragraph that evokes the real origin of her 'candle-light' aesthetic:

> I'm sitting up in bed, with the window beside me open – no matter if it's to the North, and not to the East. It's broad moonlight, and very blue. These nights when I'm sitting in Mother's room I am content enough to come in here after she settles for the night. For with the door shut and the window open one has a curious sense partly of one's own 'integrity', and partly of the wideness of the world. I sometimes write my letters this way, for candle-light is the best light for letters, as well as for most things. I always go to bed by candle-light. It's such a quiet light, and an old.

The remainder is taken up with personal messages and wishes.

On 5 January 1919, Waddell tells Taylor that she has 'just signed the [publishers'] agreement for the *Spoiled Buddha*', and also that she is considering sending them the four articles on Ballygowan House, for a separate pamphlet, though in fact she never did so. She had, she tells her correspondent, thought of putting them together with her writings on Japan, but decided against this in the end. Her standard for such compilations lies in certain books by Robert Louis Stevenson:

> Some things in *Memories and Portraits* always jarred, I think: while the essays in *Virginibus Puerisque*, diverse as they are, do flow together. Maude [Clarke] insists, I think rightly, that they would ruin the flavour of the Japanese book, when some day it comes to be collected.

She reveals also that Gregory Smith has been helping her revise the play, and how she still values his advice. But at the end of her next letter to India, on 11 January, she qualifies what she has said a little further:

> Another thing – that absurd 'Collected Works' was sheer divilment [*sic*] – I believe it was Gregory's phrase in the first instance, and is a specimen of the delightful solemnity with which he pokes fun at you. It's the dreadful contrast between the few contents I have to show, and the massive promise of the title that pleased his peculiar humour. If

> ever the book is written it will probably be called by the name of one of the essays – possibly *The Hyacinth Fields* or *The Uttermost Isles.*

'The Uttermost Isles' came out in *Asia*, with illustrations by a Japanese artist, in April 1919. After a difficult winter with her stepmother, Waddell felt more hopeful in the spring, and wrote to Taylor on 4 May:

> And I'm here working a little at – you will love to hear it – *White Iris.* When it's finished I shall try *Harper's*, I think. There is no essential change, except that the 'first person' is gone. I always felt that 'I' made the story too self-conscious. Now it's one Elizabeth, Billy's twin.

At the same time she tells him how her ideas for research are reviving. Meanwhile, reviews by her have appeared in the *Nation* and the *New Statesman.* She is much complimented on 'The Uttermost Isles', by the editor of the magazine as much as by her readers, yet, as summer approaches, the publication of her play is still delayed. Before it appears, the same publisher issues the *Poems of Roger Casement*, and this brings a surprising letter of disapproval from India. Waddell writes back defensively on 19 August and shows herself to be politically well-informed, as she tries to persuade her mentor that the small publishing house is not 'a nest of conspiracy and sedition'. 'But let's escape', she implores him. 'The whole question smothers me. Anyhow, all politics deject me unutterably, perhaps because my heart is invariably on the losing side.' Few of their letters had dealt directly with the great events that were sweeping both Ireland and the Continent throughout the 1910s. Inevitably, perhaps, Casement's name appeared in an advertisement on the back cover of the play when it finally came out. Waddell tries to dispel her mentor's disappointment before she finishes her letter:

> But dear, I wish you had liked the play better. It struck you as flippant: to me it's tragedy, far more tragic than the article in the 'M.G.' which you prefer. I know I've read far more into it than the slightness of the play will stand. But it's there for me: and for a very few other people. I don't know whether any of the reviews will see that it's more than a skit. Again, I know that it's daring to make the bronze images move and speak: but it's part of the preposterousness of the conception that these images are indeed the Buddha and Binzuru and Daruma, flesh and blood transmuted into rigidity by the impassive years. I think the thought at the back of the play is that the narrow way of ascesis attracts either the finest natures or the weeds – narrow ill-minded people like Daruma, or great rich natures like the Buddha's. Binzuru

> has his possibilities, but the way is too high for him: his rich humanity is not high enough for perseverance in the way. And the life in the outer court though it has made him a kindly god has coarsened him – withal, it is *life*, 'the passionate and humorous life of men' that comes before the Buddha at the last: he all but yields to it, having found the emptyness of Nirvana: but tradition is too strong. I *think* it is tradition. For the Buddha by this time knows that one finds the infinite here also.

For the rest of the year, however, even as Waddell plans further work and sends off her reviews, the background noise of Irish politics forms a low grumble to her exchanges with Taylor.

As the year turns again, articles by Waddell appear in the *Nation* with increasing regularity, while her domestic situation grows more burdensome and trying. Yet the memory of Japan still has the power to provoke in her quite vivid, sensual recollection. Addressing a book by Arthur Waley, this time of poems from Japan, she finds room for some of her thoughts about Japanese poetry, 'so tiny in content, so infinite in suggestion', though her essay on that subject was never written. She also shows how her perception of the world continues to be refracted through her childhood experiences in the East: 'Flowering currant in February has the essence of August afternoons: it can turn a railway siding on a bleak Antrim coast into the Pilgrims' Road to Kamakura, pungent with the smell of pines and the hot, white bitterness of dust.'[88]

In March, the same month that this appears, however, she makes her final contribution to the missionary journal *Daybreak*. Undoubtedly this curtailing of her activities had something to do with the news just now reaching her of Taylor's death. His last letter to her, written on 16 February, had described the symptoms of his illness and informed her of the legacy that she would receive. As before, we do not know exactly when the letter came, but with his death, on 21 February 1920, Waddell's connection with Asia broke permanently. In June her stepmother Martha also died, setting her free to leave Belfast. Not much later she decided to give up the narrow little house where she had been so unhappy for almost a decade. From then on, except for occasional flickering references in articles or letters, she never wrote in any substantial way about Japan or other aspects of the East again. Instead, her life began anew elsewhere, in Oxford and Paris and London, and although her reviewing continued briefly, it was soon displaced by the Latin scholarship that eventually made her famous.

This early body of writing by Helen Waddell on subjects connected with Japan has several noticeable features, foremost among them the apparent singleness of her preoccupation with her brother Billy. From her private correspondence we know the reasons for her concern and have observed how Billy and his difficulties seem to underlie even writings in which he is not mentioned or described directly. Indeed, Billy and Japan appear to be almost coterminous as subjects for Waddell in this decade of her life in Belfast. Her impulse to write about her brother receives its clearest expression in two undated pages of her letters to Taylor. These stray pages form the last part of an incomplete letter evidently written in the middle period of their exchanges, after she had revealed the truth about Billy to her mentor, and probably before she started work on her literary essays. Here Waddell writes:

> And away at the back of my mind I am seeing a glimmering of what I think my *real* book will some day be. I have been thinking a good deal of Billy: the ugly mouth and the most beautiful smile I ever saw; the queerest mixture of sensuousness and imagination, spirit and flesh, religion and devilry. And I suddenly knew that some day I was going to write of Billy the child: all the promise that flickered out; Billy, before he was 'Derelict, Dangerous to Navigation,' as he once said of himself. The richest thing in my life has been Japan – outside books, I mean: but I could not bear to do myself in Japan, I'd be too self-conscious: but I can put all myself into Billy, for he *was* like me. It will be a child's East, with its delight and its strangeness and its sinister breath: I know from things I remember that Billy saw that sinister evil side of it with the same half-attraction, half-repulsion that he found in drugs. The book will end, I think, with the boy suddenly diving back from the rail where he was waving goodbye to my father in the little sampan, because he was ashamed to cry. You know, Billy and Geo. came home to school alone; a Japanese ship with a kindly English captain and a sneering devil of a Scottish engineer… Some of the stuff I have written already will go into it. It mayn't be written for years. But I think it will be some day. And it will be Billy's Apologia.

This is abundantly clear about Helen's desire to redeem, or exculpate, her wayward brother. The last paragraphs refer to Taylor's obituary for Meta Fleming and to Waddell's work on the story of Hasan of El Basrah, so that the letter must have been written in the spring of 1917.

In the absence of any record of Waddell's immediate response either to the knowledge of her brother's drug addiction or to the news about his death, we can only speculate about such matters. However, some of her deeper thinking can be construed from the considered remarks that she makes to Taylor later. Describing Billy's problems in the letter of 30 May 1916 quoted above, Waddell refers to an essay by Robert Louis Stevenson called ‘Old Mortality’. This piece, which appeared in Stevenson’s *Memories and Portraits* (1881), is essentially a meditation on life and death in the form of reflections by the author in a Scottish graveyard. It is the third part that Waddell quotes in her letter, where Stevenson writes about a man who ‘somewhere on the high seas of life, with his health, his hopes, his patrimony, and his self-respect, miserably went down’. Almost every sentence of this four-page passage of reminiscence resonates strangely with regard to Billy Waddell, and we can only think that Helen must have meditated deeply on it: ‘a man, by his own fault ruined; shut out from the garden of his gifts; his whole city of hope both ploughed and salted; silently awaiting the deliverer’.

The letters that elucidate Waddell’s thinking at this time, and reveal the genesis of her stories in the facts of her biography, are mainly those that she wrote to Taylor. These were preserved by his widow and most of them have come down to us complete. This is not the case with the letters that Waddell received from India, few of which have survived undamaged and only two of which do not have missing pages. Waddell’s niece, Miss Mollie Martin, believes that Waddell mutilated or destroyed many of her personal papers in later life during the onset of the disease which ravaged her mental faculties. The surviving letters more often lack their opening than their closing pages and are consequently difficult to date. Some have been cut away, or else marked with lines down the left-hand margin for emphasis, though the reasons for this are not always clear. A few passages have been crossed through diagonally once, obviously to delete the contents, though again it is not clear why. Some more precise deletions, made to a letter of Taylor’s dated 25 June 1916, are, however, highly significant. This is the letter that he wrote in response to the one in which Waddell had opened her heart to him about Billy’s drug addiction. Taylor writes back to console and reassure her, but every mention of Billy’s name in this letter has been scored through, and above most a line of three asterisks has been inserted. One whole sentence that refers to Billy has also been scored out. That such defacement, whenever it occurred, represents an emotional response by Waddell, probably of anger or regret, is not to be doubted and is further evidence of her deep involvement with her brother.

The fact that only Helen chose to write about her childhood in Japan and not her older brother Samuel, the other renowned author in the family, can perhaps be explained by the different circumstances of their lives. Samuel Waddell was the fourth of the sons and, like all the children except the eldest, was born in Japan. He lived there until about the age of ten when he was sent back to Ireland to be educated. In adult life he trained as a surveyor and worked for the Irish Land Commission. He also acted and wrote plays under the name ‘Rutherford Mayne’, and was one

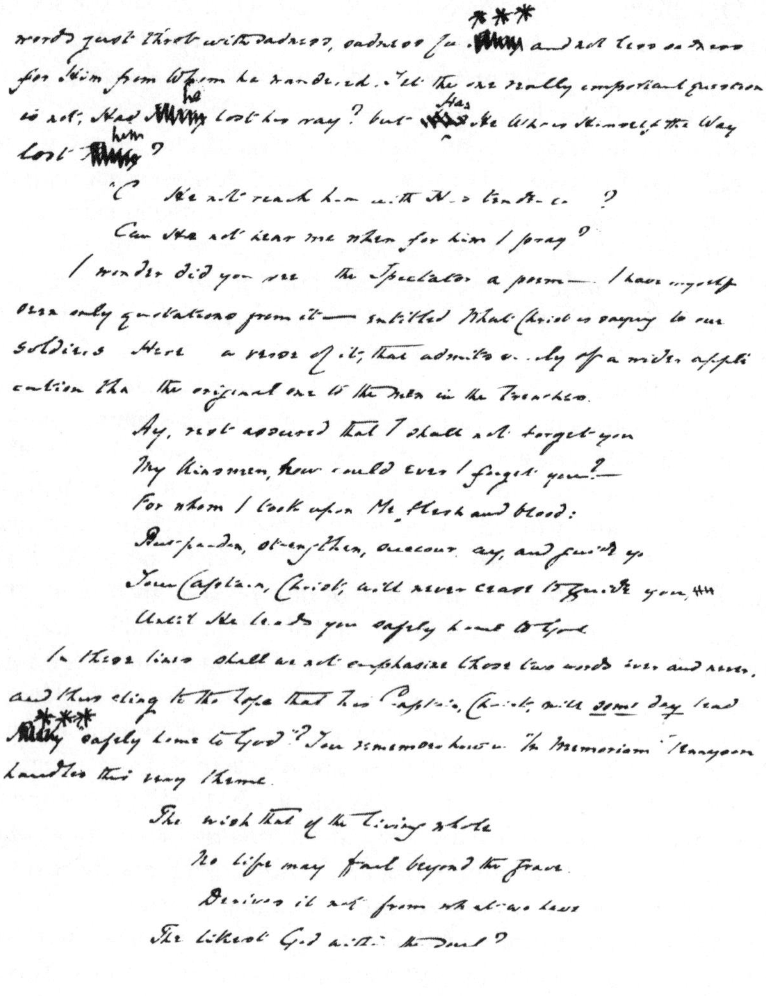

words just throb with sadness, sadness for *** [redacted] and not less sadness for Him from Whom he wandered. Still the one really important question is not, Had he [redacted] lost his way? but Has He Who is Himself the Way lost him [redacted]?

"O Can He not reach him with His tenderness?
Can He not hear me when for him I pray?"

I wonder did you see in the Spectator a poem — I have myself seen only quotations from it — entitled What Christ is saying to our soldiers. Here is a verse of it, that admits only of a wider application than the original one to the men in the Trenches.

Ay, rest assured that I shall not forget you
My kinsmen, how could ever I forget you? —
For whom I took upon Me flesh and blood:
[illegible], strengthen, succour, ay, and guide you
Your Captain, Christ, will never cease to guide you,
Until He leads you safely home to God

In these lines shall we not emphasize those two words ever and never, and thus cling to the hope that his Captain, Christ, will some day lead *** [redacted] safely home to God? You remember how in "In Memoriam" Tennyson handles this very theme.

The wish that of the living whole
No life may fail beyond the grave
Derives it not from what we have
The likest God within the soul?

Dr Taylor's letter of consolation, scored through by Helen Waddell.

of the founding members of the Ulster Literary Theatre. Yet, in spite of having spent almost twice as long in Japan as his younger sister Helen, he appears to have written nothing about this. Only in his last play, *Bridge Head* (1939), do we find any reference to Japan, and even then it seems only to be a sort of bemused 'signature' to the work, in the form of a Japanese character whose presence is not essential to its meaning.[89] For Helen, particularly in her early writing, her background in Japan is a taproot, something central to her imaginative world, while for her brother it is a largely incidental matter. Part of the reason for this difference undoubtedly lies in the difference in their lives. Samuel Waddell belonged to the outward world of men and business, dealing with affairs that provided him with material for dramatic work. His life was relatively unrestricted and afforded many satisfactions. Helen's life, on the other hand, was one of considerable restriction and frustration, particularly since she had to stay at home through her twenties to look after her stepmother. Helen also found few opportunities in the academic life of Belfast, though she was not free to leave the city until she had passed the age of 30. Thwarted in her external life, she had no choice perhaps but to turn inward, to rely on memory and imagination in her writing, and to depend for the remainder on her reading. Japan was almost the only part of her real life that had been imaginatively satisfying and offered her fulfilment 'outside books'.

While Helen Waddell's stories about her childhood in Japan, and especially her sister Margaret's teenage diary, have some historical value for their joint portrait of the lives of missionary children in the Meiji period, the important difference between them is that what Helen wrote is actually fiction. We have seen how she shaped and reworked selected incidents from her childhood so that her stories must be appraised, not only for their historical, but also for their artistic, value. Her urge to recreate her childhood is deeply informed by a sense of loss. This is hardly surprising if we consider that, after returning from Japan the first time, her natural mother had died, and that after the lost setting of her infancy had been restored, it was then removed again, and that her father died soon afterwards as well. The sense of irretrievable loss she evidently felt for the locations of her childhood, including Ballygowan House in County Down, and the nostalgia with which she retrospectively evokes them, suggest a parallel with another Belfast writer, her senior and contemporary Forrest Reid (1875–1947).

'The primary impulse of the artist springs, I fancy, from discontent, and his art is a kind of crying for Elysium', says Reid in the opening paragraph of his autobiography of childhood, *Apostate* (1926). As it happened, both he and Helen Waddell came from Presbyterian stock and neither seems to have found the city they inhabited satisfying to their imaginative needs. Reid describes Belfast in *Apostate* as 'a rather hard, unromantic town … devoted exclusively to money-making', just as Waddell still remembered late in life the 'thin red brick house' where she had lived unhappily with her stepmother. Both writers responded to the shortcomings of the world around them by creating in their work a more desirable elsewhere, but where Reid took refuge in a dream of ancient Greece, Waddell was able to draw upon her recollections of a real Japan. The romanticised, and partly fictional, world that she creates in her early writing also calls to mind the 'blue remembered hills' of Shropshire in the poetry of A.E. Housman (1859–1936), who likewise evokes the past nostalgically: 'That is the land of lost content, / I see it shining plain, / The happy highways where I went / And cannot go again.'[90] All three writers were to some extent marginalised by their sexuality (Waddell as a woman, Reid as a paedophile, Housman as a homosexual), which probably contributed to their need for an alternative, romantic world. But Waddell's comment, in 'The Hyacinth Fields', that 'every bend in the river is a grateful thing to those of us who are for ever threatened with the canal', also suggests a late-Romantic rejection of the practical and business world on aesthetic grounds.

'Oh all this feminine orientalism!' remarks the poet and novelist George Buchanan (1904–89), a younger friend of, both Reid and Waddell, in exasperation in his autobiography. He then asks himself, 'Why in Ulster do we hanker for it so?'[91] It is true that Buchanan is thinking here of Reid, rather than of Helen Waddell. But the question still arises as to whether a romantic, orientalising tendency can be found particularly in Irish writers of Protestant extraction. It can certainly be observed, among writers born in Ulster, in the work of the mystical poet and reformer 'A.E.' (George Russell, 1867–1935), a friend of Helen Waddell when she later lived in England, as well as in that of the Theosophical Belfast poet James H. Cousins (1873–1956). In Waddell's case, however, her interest in, and knowledge of the East were not assumed in adulthood, but had grown naturally out of her own experience. Thus, although her Eastern subject matter seems to connect her with the tradition of orientalism in English literature, the fact that what she writes about derives from firsthand experience must also be borne in mind. Like Rudyard Kipling in India, Waddell had been born in the country that she wrote about and spoke the language of that country when she lived there. This cannot be viewed simply as cultural appropriation, since childhood experience is an ineradicable part of any adult. It is true that Waddell had been born to missionary parents and that the goal of missionaries is to displace the religion of another country with their own. Yet in spite of this, she movingly and sympathetically portrays aspects of Japanese religion in her stories.

Although Waddell did not write about Japan after she left Belfast, she still cherished her memories of living there. Her biographer notes how images of Japan continued to affect her views of places that she encountered later in her life. On a holiday in Italy in 1921, she writes excitedly to share the new places that she is seeing with her sister. 'Just before we left Venice', she reports on 8 April, 'the wisteria had begun to come out, and it was queer to see it again after such years – made me suddenly hanker for Tokio.' And there are other reminders.[92] Viewing a house in London in 1925, she once more writes in detail about it to her sister: 'I don't know

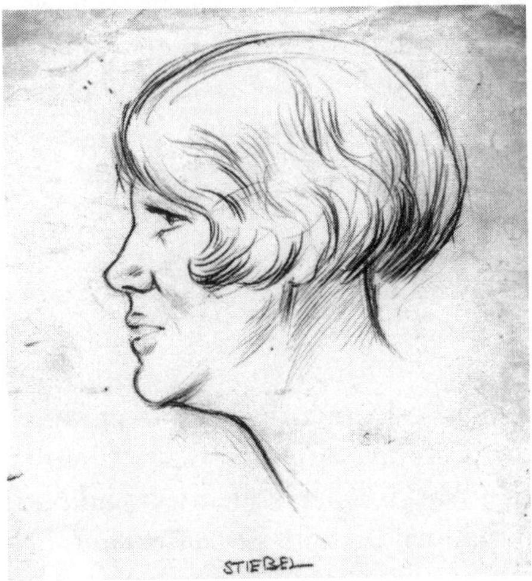

The scholar Helen Waddell.

price or anything, but I sat awhile on the verandah steps and invented freely … For a minute it was like Japan.'[93] It is almost as if the degree to which such places evoke her childhood in Japan becomes the affective measure of her response to them. We can also observe how such images re-echo in her writing.

The 'bend in the river' motif, which figures centrally in 'The Hyacinth Fields', is a good example, not only of the romantic slant to her imagination, but also of the way that such an image is evolved within it. She first refers to this image in a letter to Taylor, quoted above, on 27 June 1916, in which she describes the picture on a Japanese fan: 'a glimpse of a bay, and then a headland with pines on it, and behind it one knows there is a smaller bay, for the shore juts out again'. In the letter she connects the picture directly with her memories of Kamakura. But the image she now carries in her mind has already diverged somewhat from the place where the Waddells actually stayed. The next year, at work on her essay on Chinese poets, Helen writes to Taylor on 2 December about some lyrics from Japan that make her think of Billy, and once more, as we have seen, invokes that 'hidden bay between two headlands'. In the completed essay it is absorbed into the Chinese story of the lost upper reaches of the river, and then a general poetic theory, and finally Waddell's light assertion that 'the idea of the bend is surely the peculiar property of the East'. Again she mentions 'the unseen bay between two pine-fringed headlands', and what is out of sight beyond. By now the headland image has become, in the developing motif, not just a prompt for nostalgic recollection, but more than that, the locus of all dreams and imagination. The appeal this image had for Waddell seems to be further demonstrated by its reappearance in her last significant new piece of writing, some thirty years after this early essay. In a translation from Petronius that she includes in her W.P. Ker Memorial Lecture of 28 October 1947, one passage runs:

> The fretted seas he sent this way and that
> With his great-bellied keels: if round yon headland
> A little bay lay hid, or distant land
> That cropped with gold, she was the enemy.[94]

The drift of this portion is that the rapacious Romans wished to conquer and exploit every last corner of the earth. While other translators render the yet undiscovered as a 'hidden bay', Waddell has added a 'headland' that secludes the 'little bay' in wording that echoes both her letters and her essay. If we do identify it in this way, then Waddell is still invoking in this late translation memories of her childhood half a century before.

The story of Billy, like other motifs in Waddell's early writing, finds echoes in her later work as well. There are strange reminders of him in the chapter she writes on the brilliant and debauched Archpoet in *The Wandering Scholars* (1927), as well as in her notes on that poet in the accompanying *Mediaeval Latin Lyrics* (1929). There is only one reference to Japan in the former volume, but significantly it is to the 'Feast of Lanterns', a popular name in English for the Bon festival or Feast of the Dead, held in summer.[95] Orpheus's loss of Eurydice, a central image in Waddell's final essay on Japan, re-emerges in a poem by Boethius translated by her in the latter volume, while the line from Milton that she quoted in that essay had already reappeared in the final pages of the former volume. The discussion of sinners in Book I of her novel *Peter Abelard* (1933),[96] inevitably calls to mind the story of Binzuru and, beyond that, of Waddell's brother Billy. The idea of reunion with the dead that 'The Uttermost Isles' explores, resonates further when we remember that Héloise had the body of Peter Abelard brought to her for burial, and was herself later buried next to him.[97]

Altogether, it is perhaps not unreasonable, in view of the thematic resemblance between Waddell's early play *The Spoiled Buddha* and her mature novel *Peter Abelard*, to suppose that the central impulse of her whole creative output may have derived from her concern with Billy. The prodigal son Billy easily transmutes into the wayward disciple Binzuru, and then Abelard the wayward cleric. Waddell herself provides a hint of this connection in her last public remarks, a radio talk about her novel that was apparently delivered in 1955. Monica Blackett reprints the text of this as it was read by Waddell, who tells us that she decided to write 'a book on Abelard and Héloise' in the spring of 1913.[98] If we consider that this was not long after she had learnt about Billy's problem with drugs, and had begun to write about him, then it does not seem inconceivable that the novel is connected with these things. But the idea that they may have been linked together deep in her imagination, the one engendering the other, to issue in a mature artistic work after twenty years' gestation, must remain speculative.

There can be no question, however, that it is her brother Billy who dominates Helen Waddell's writings on Japan, from the happy childhood stories, through the agonising of her Buddhist play, to the last essay in which she evidently mourns his death. That subject matter from Japan served to enrich her first literary work is also beyond doubt. Like Milton, Waddell was haunted by the thought of wasting the literary gift that had been vouchsafed her, although until she had passed the age of 30 she could only 'stand and wait'. Her own claim, in a letter quoted at the outset, provides the best summation of her first attempts at writing in the 1910s: 'The richest thing in my life has been Japan – outside books, I mean.' Yet it was the rider to this statement that indicated where her future lay.

Notes

Introduction

1 The most accessible accounts of Hugh Waddell's life are in the obituary notices given in the *Proceedings of the General Conference of Protestant Missionaries in Japan Held in Tokyo October, 24–31, 1900* (Tokyo: Methodist Publishing House, 1901), pp. 976–8; and in *The Japan Evangelist* (Tokyo), 8: 10 (Oct. 1901), pp. 302–6, where a notice reprinted from the *Belfast Witness* is supplemented by part of the *Proceedings* (1901) notice. The same volume of *Proceedings* also contains Revd G.F. Verbeck's detailed 'History of Protestant Missions in Japan to 1883', first presented at the general conference of 1883, and which refers to Hugh Waddell and his work in the appropriate sections. For the subsequent period, 1883–1900, the summaries are general and contain no specific references. Further information about him can be found, in Japanese, in *Meiji Gakuin Hyaku-nen-shi* [A Hundred-Year History of Meiji Gakuin] (Tokyo: Meiji Gakuin, 1976), pp. 20–1, 40–3; and in *Nihon Kirisuto-kyō Rekishi Daijiten* [Dictionary of Christian History in Japan] (Tokyo: Kyo Bun Kwan, 1988), p. 1547.

2 G.B. Sansom, *The Western World and Japan* (New York: Knopf, 1970; first published 1950), p. 470.

3 See Edward Seidensticker, *High City, Low City* (New York: Knopf, 1983), pp.36–42.

4 Quoted in *The Japan Evangelist*, pp. 303–4. The visitor was from Ireland.

5 It accords roughly with Roppongi 3-chōme in Tokyo today.

6 *Proceedings* (1901), pp. 809, 832.

7 It is not mentioned in the detailed listings of such schools of all Protestant denominations, including those no longer in operation, given in H. Ritter's *History of Protestant Missions in Japan* (Tokyo: Methodist Publishing House, 1898), pp. 371–85.

8 See the Registration Letters of Meiji Gakuin, p. 31. The address is given as Ichibee-chō, Azabu-ku, which maps of the time indicate as being adjacent to Fukide-chō.

9 *Proceedings* (1901), p. 862.

10 None is specifically attributed to him in the summary of this work by Dr Hepburn, the head of the original committee appointed in 1876. See *Uemura Masahisa to Sono Jidai* [Uemura Masahisa and His Times], ed. Sawa Wataru (Tokyo: Kyo Bun Kwan, 1938), vol. 4, pp. 120–8. This portion of the text is in English, but there are extensive references to Hugh Waddell in the records of committee work, vols. 1–5, *passim.*

11 'The Influence of Chinese Literature as an Obstacle to the Reception of Christianity in Japan' in *Proceedings* (1883), pp. 106–17.

12 *Proceedings* (1901), p. 976.

13 For an introduction to the field see, for example, Par Barr, *The Coming of the Barbarians: A Story of Western Settlement in Japan 1853–1870* (London: Macmillan, 1967) and *The*

Deer Cry Pavilion: A Story of Westerners in Japan 1868–1905 (London: Macmillan, 1968), or Hugh Cortazzi, *Victorians in Japan: In and around the Treaty Ports* (London: Athlone Press, 1987).

14 Though Helen's older brother Samuel, the only other member of this large family to become a writer, appears to have written nothing about his childhood in Japan and had probably returned to Ireland before she was born.

15 *Kipling's Japan: Collected Writings*, edited by Hugh Cortazzi and George Webb (London: Athlone Press, 1988), p. 190.

16 Clara A.N. Whitney, *Clara's Diary: An American Girl in Meiji Japan*, ed. M. William Steel and Tamiko Ichimata (Tokyo: Kodansha International, 1979).

17 See Felicitas Corrigan, *Helen Waddell: A Biography* (London: Gollancz, 1986), p. 19. The story was related to the biographer by Waddell's niece Miss Mollie Martin.

18 It was from there that he wrote to his family, ibid., p. 21.

19 *Handbook for Travellers in Japan*, 3rd edn, 'Revised and for the most part re-written' by Basil Hall Chamberlain and W.B. Mason (London: John Murray, 1891), p. 73. As the wording on the title-page suggests, this was a new edition of an earlier book compiled by different authors.

20 Kate M. Youngman (1841–1910), an American missionary who went to Japan in 1873, started the Ueno mission in 1890, later worked with lepers and died in Japan. See *Nihon Kirisuto-kyō Rekishi Daijiten*, p. 1450.

21 The details are given by Corrigan, *Helen Waddell*, p. 25. The biographer also gives select, sometimes conflated, extracts. The address corresponds approximately to Roppongi 3-chōme in Tokyo today.

22 Margaret refers in the diary to her stepmother's bed, but is otherwise unclear.

23 Diary, *passim*. Some of the flowers and vegetables are not native to Japan, and were either imported varieties or approximate names for indigenous plants.

24 Edward Seidensticker, *High City, Low City: Tokyo from Edo to the Earthquake* (New York: Knopf, 1983), p. 127.

25 Wada Shūhō (1854–1946), who was trained by Hugh and took over in his absence. He went on to have a distinguished career in both the church and public service. See *Nihon Kirisuto-kyō Rekishi Daijiten*, pp. 1541–2.

26 She does not record this in the diary, but it is evident from a beautifully illustrated Japanese children's *kana* or syllabary study book that was preserved by her daughter Mollie Martin. Margaret has written her name on the back, which is the front of a Japanese book, and makes some errors in her pencilled transliterations. This book is now in the editor's possession. See p. 16.

27 See Corrigan, *Helen Waddell*, Ch. 1.

28 Chamberlain and Mason, *Handbook for Travellers in Japan*, p. 55.

29 Verses from it are used as epigraphs for the first chapters of his novel *Kim*. The main sights of Kamakura have all been preserved, though the town is much larger today.

30 It was brought out by Constable, enjoyed modest success and was several times reprinted.

31 See Corrigan, *Helen Waddell*, pp. 103–5 and Monica Blackett *The Mark of the Maker: A Portrait of Helen Waddell* (London: Constable, 1973), pp. 24–8. In fact, Waddell used another source for some of the later poems, as the book acknowledges.

32 For the dating of the letter, see David Burleigh, 'The Early Writings of Helen Waddell on Japan: A Survey and Interpretation' (M.Phil. thesis, University of Sussex, 2000), p. 24.

33 The magazine was *Blackwoods*, in which her work never actually appeared.

34 On 23 July 1898, Margaret records: 'In evening Mr. Takahashi (Kam. Evan.) came to see us.'

35 In the handwritten version of this story Helen Waddell has actually written Youngman, then crossed it out and added the other name. She may have been conscious of the fact that the people she was writing about were still alive. Miss Youngman was an occasional visitor to the Waddells' home in Tokyo, and even the mild-natured Margaret has occasion to record her as being 'irritable' (29 July 1898), and again as someone her father is 'disgusted with' (9 July 1900).

36 The first is to the 'maternal orders in council' at the beginning of 'After Strange Gods'; the second occurs towards the end of 'The White Iris', when 'their mother found that [the rickshaw man] had two children and gave him the persimmons the twins had meant to eat…'

37 Revd. T. Alfred Large was a Canadian Methodist who went to Japan with his wife in 1885. He was murdered by armed intruders at their home in 1890. Mrs Large stayed on and worked for the Women's Christian Temperance Union. See *Proceedings* (1901), pp. 137–8, 712; also *Tōyō Eiwa Jogakuin Hyaku-nen-shi* [A Hundred-Year History of Tōyō Eiwa Girls' School] (Tokyo: Tôyô Eiwa Jogakuin, 1984), pp. 52–9; and A.H. Ion, *The Cross and the Rising Sun* (Waterloo, Ontario: Wlifred Laurier University Press, 1990), pp. xxi, 30, 107, 126 for photographs and further details. A surviving school report of Helen's shows that she attended Tōyō Eiwa Girls' School.

38 3 March 1898. This is the day of the *Hina Matsuri* or Dolls' Festival, a special day for girls in Japan, but there is no mention of this. Margaret carefully observed New Year's decorations on their neighbours' houses, but clearly few of the native customs were brought inside the Waddells' home.

39 The only place in Margaret's diary in which Helen appears next to her brother Billy is in a sketch that Margaret made of the four youngest children running down a hill, with the caption 'Me Geo Wil Hel run down the peak'. It appears in the entry for 18 May 1900, but may have been done earlier.

40 See *The Campbell College Register 1894–1938*, Campbell College, Belfast. The fact that both boys were in the Lower Sixth at the same time suggests that they entered the same academic year.

41 He was granted a Licentiate of the Royal College of Surgeons and the Royal College of Physicians, both of Edinburgh, and of the Royal Faculty of Physicians and Surgeons of Glasgow. Taking a qualification under the auspices of the Scottish Board was apparently a cheaper way of doing it than by enrolling at Queen's College full-time. The registration document, written in the applicant's own hand, states 'Matriculation R.U.I. [Royal University of Ireland]', though no record has turned up in Dublin to confirm this.

42 There is no record of her graduation.

43 The hospital in which Billy was a patient, Haydock Lodge, was 'a private asylum for the restoration and cure of the insane', located at Haydock in Lancashire, not far from Liverpool. It was opened in 1843 and closed in 1970. The records up to 1908 only are so far available for public inspection.

44 *Stories from Holy Writ* (London: Constable, 1949), p. ix. The note of disdain is unmistakable, and even the colophon says 'Kilmacrew House, 1914', giving the name of her sister's home in County Down, although nearly all of the writing had been done in Belfast.

45 This title was later dropped, in part probably because what Waddell wrote tended to become too difficult for the intended audience of infants. Her name was later given

as 'Helen Waddell, M.A.'

46 See the entry dated 14 October 1899, which describes a visit to a temple in Shiba Park. This one-page entry is the only one made in the diary between 8 July 1899 and the end of that year. This was the period when Billy and George left Japan to return to Ireland. In January 1900 the diarist begins anew, with regular and detailed entries.

47 Isabella L. Bird, *Unbeaten Tracks in Japan: An Account of Travels in the Interior* (London: John Murray, 2nd edn, 1880), vol. I, p. 69.

48 Ibid., pp. 66, 69–70. Letter VIII deals with the visit to Asakusa. The official name of the temple is Sensōji.

49 William M. Imbrie, who was known to the Waddells and appears in Margaret's diary, gives the height of the statue as 'perhaps two feet', in *The Church of Christ in Japan: A Course of Lectures* (Philadelphia: Westminster Press, 1906), p. 17.

50 *Clara's Diary*, Clara A.N. Whitney, p. 35.

51 *Handbook for Travellers in Japan*, p. 28. The information about Binzuru is taken over from the previous edition: 'The seated image to the r., with a pink and yellow cloth bib round his neck, and now almost rubbed away with age, was a celebrated work of Jikaku Dai-shi, and represents Bindzuru, the helper of the sick (Sanskr. Pi*n*dola). This is one of the Sixteen Arhat (Jiū-roku Rakan) … According to popular Japanese tradition, [Binzuru] was expelled from the Sixteen for having violated his vow of chastity by remarking upon the beauty of a woman, and hence his usual situation outside the temple [chancel]. It is also said that the Buddha conferred on him at his special request the power of curing all human ills.' Ernest Mason Satow and A.G.S. Hawes, *A Handbook for Travellers in Northern and Central Japan* (London: John Murray, 2nd edn, 1884), p. 30. In Waddell's version of the story Binzuru does not request the powers that he is granted by the Buddha.

52 The story is mentioned in 'The Uttermost Isles', and again in Waddell's study *The Wandering Scholars* (London: Constable, 1990; first published 1927), p. 140.

53 Japanese sources confirm this, but are not specific about the way his powers were misused, or the exact cause of his downfall. See, for example, Ishida Mizumaro, *Reibun Bukkyō Daijiten* [Illustrative Encylopaedia of Buddhism] (Tokyo: Shogakkan, 1997), p. 911.

54 See Charles Eliot, *Japanese Buddhism* (London: Routledge & Kegan Paul, 1935), p. 137.

55 Daruma, or Bodhidharma, was a sixth-century saint, who went from India to China, where he established the meditative form of Buddhism. He is believed to have lost his legs from excessive meditation, which caused them to wither and drop off. As Daruma, he is a popular figure in Japan today, often reproduced as a papier mâché doll.

56 Chamberlain and Mason describe Kwannon as the 'Goddess of Mercy', and then add off-handedly: 'According to another but less popular opinion, Kwannon belongs to the male sex' (*Handbook for Travellers in Japan*, p. 28). Isabella Bird also has a footnote to the effect that Kannon is actually male, *Unbeaten Tracks in Japan*, vol. I, p. 62.

57 The bodhisattva is an enlightened soul on the way to Nirvana. In the case of Avalokitesvara, as Kwannon [Kannon] was originally known, his being neither male nor female is particularly stressed. Another Belfast writer, the poet James Cousins (1873–1956), who visited Japan in 1919–20 and died in India, gives a more accurate account in this stanza from his poem 'A Tibetan Banner':

A thousand thousand years ago,
On a great mountain tipped with snow,
Born of the giant Earthquake's pains

Between Tibet and India's plains
Lived Avalokiteswara.
Invisible incognita;
Man-woman grown to God-estate,
Pure, passionless, compassionate;
Set on the sacred lotus-seat
With blessing hands and folded feet;
Dwelling in meditative mood
Upon the verge of Buddhahood.

Collected Poems (Adyar, Madras: Kalākshetra, 1940), p. 310. Cousins poetically exaggerates the time of Avalokitesvara's existence, which is not known.

58 Gilbert and Sullivan's 1885 opera was merely the high point in a late-Victorian fashion for stories of Japan in British theatre. See 'Japan on the Stage' in Earl Miner, *The Japanese Tradition in British and American Literature* (Westport, CT: Greenwood Press, 1976; first published 1958), pp. 52–61.

59 The Belfast Opera House was opened in 1895 with an exotic interior created from a mixture of oriental styles. *The Spoiled Buddha* was presented there for a week from 1 February, preceded on alternate days by one of two different comedies. See *The Belfast News Letter* (30 Jan. 1915), p. 1.

60 The review of the first night in *The Belfast News Letter* (2 Feb. 1915), p. 6, largely agrees.

61 'The temple of Kuanon at Asakusa is to Tōkiō what St. Paul's is to London, or Nôtre Dame to Paris,' says W.E. Griffis in *The Mikado's Empire* (New York: Harper & Brothers, 1903; first published, 1876), p. 378. It was the greatest temple in Tokyo, and, like all large ones, had a busy market and all kinds of entertainment in its grounds. For the Yoshiwara itself, see J.E. de Becker's classic study, *The Nightless City, or the History of the Yoshiwara Yūkwaku* (New York & Tokyo: ICG Muse, 2000; first published 1899), which first appeared anonymously.

62 In one of Helen's letters to her sister, dated simply 'Friday night', she alludes to this: 'I went to see Mrs. Taylor… She was awfully keen that I should go back with her for a year…' But the care of her stepmother made this impossible. 'It is nice to think about', she ruefully observes to Margaret.

63 For details of Taylor's visit, see *The Missionary Herald* (Belfast) 1 May 1914, p. 106; 1 Jan. 1915, p. 8.

64 Return of deaths at sea for December 1914 (Ref. BT 334/63) and official log book No. 6 of S.S. *Derbyshire* (Ref. BT 165/704), pp. 26–8 (Public Record Office).

65 Bird, vol. I, p. 254.

66 The others are 'Seisin', published in the *Manchester Guardian* (29 Dec. 1915), and 'Dead – and Buried', ibid. (3 Dec. 1917). As always they were back page articles. The fourth piece, 'Religio Loci', seems never to have been published.

67 He was also engaged to be married, and was visiting his fiançée when it happened.

68 *The Princess Splendour and Other Stories*, by Helen Waddell, ed., Eileen Colwell (London: Longman, 1969), p. 9.

69 *Princess Splendor: The Wood-cutter's Daughter*, trans. E. Rothesay Miller (Tokyo: Kobunsha, 1889). The original tale is anonymous.

70 Waddell, *The Princess Splendour*, p. 39.

71 *The "Kojiki": Records of Ancient Matters*, trans. Basil Hall Chamberlain (Tokyo: Charles E. Tuttle, 1981; first published 1882) pp. 145–56. Chamberlain is credited as a source for 'The Uttermost Isles' below. Other books circulating at the time contained simplified retellings of selected episodes, frequently for children. For further detail on

Waddell's other sources, both likely and confirmed, see Burleigh, 'The Early Writings of Helen Waddell on Japan', pp. 58–70.

72 See Mrs Hugh Fraser [Mary Crawford Fraser], *A Diplomatist's Wife in Japan: Letters from Home to Home* (London: Hutchinson, 1900; first published 1899). This volume is not mentioned anywhere by Waddell, though it is possible her library contained it.

73 Waddell's tale 'The Garden of Xarifa', survives in manuscript and runs to about 5,000 words. It is based on Washington Irving's 'Legend of Prince Ahmed al Kamel', found in his book *Alhambra*. A bowdlerised version only was printed in her lifetime. See Burleigh, 'The Early Writings of Helen Waddell on Japan', Appendix II.

74 G.P. Taylor, 'Meta Fleming, M.A.' in *Woman's Work: Zenana Mission Quarterly* (Belfast) (Spring 1917). The actress Cathleen Nesbitt, who went to school with both girls, describes Meta as 'the best-loved girl in whatever class she was in', and Helen as 'the most intelligent' girl in the school (and there is a photograph of them all together) in her autobiography *A Little Love and Good Company* (London: Faber, 1975), p. 24.

75 Probably this was the same Mr Santo they had known in Japan. Margaret writes in her diary, on 6 June 1898: 'Papa and mother gone to Mr Santo's.'

76 George Saintsbury's book *The Peace of the Augustans: A Survey of Eighteenth Century Literature as a place of Rest and Refreshment*, had appeared the year before. Saintsbury chose to ignore the war in Europe in this study, parts of which were written with Helen Waddell specifically in mind. See Dorothy Richardson Jones, *'King of Critics': George Saintsbury 1845–1933* (Ann Arbor, MI: University of Michigan Press, 1992), p. 272.

77 The type of fan referred to here is probably the flat circular type with a bamboo handle (*uchiwa*), rather than the more expensive folding fan (*sensu*).

78 The book in question was *The Classical Poetry of the Japanese*, trans. by Basil Hall Chamberlain (London: Trübner, 1880).

79 This is the whole of 'Flowers and Moonlight on the Spring River' by Yang-ti in *One Hundred & Seventy Chinese Poems* translated by Arthur Waley (London: Constable, 1918).

80 Arthur Waley (1889–1966) was Helen Waddell's exact contemporary, though there is no record of their having met. Her review of his first volume of translations came out in the *Nation* on 28 September and she later reviewed several other books by him there. She was generous and enthusiastic in her comments and response. Some of his work is quoted in the early pages of Waddell's *The Wandering Scholars*.

81 'By some European writers they are supposed to be the Japan Islands: by Langlès, the Sunda Islands. But I rather think that the Arab geographers applied the name of Wák-Wák to all the islands with which they were acquainted on the east and south-east of Borneo.' The name 'Sarawak' seems to be Waddell's supposition, and is not mentioned by Lane specifically. See *The Arabian Nights' Entertainments* trans. Edward William Lane (London: Charles Knight, 1841), vol. III, p. 523. Sir Richard Burton makes no bones about the matter in a footnote to his later translation: '[Hasan of Bassorah]'s travels are in Jinn-land and Japan.' See *The Book of the Thousand Nights and a Night* trans R.F. Burton (London: H.S. Nichols, 1897, first published 1885–86), vol. VI, p. 166. The Queen's University Library, where Waddell consulted Lane, has both editions.

82 These tragedies were to be repeated, with the death of her friend Maude Clarke in the 1930s and the deaths of two of her sister Margaret's sons during World War II. See biographical accounts.

83 The poem is XXXII in the 'Lyrisches Intermezzo' sequence of his *Buch der Lieder* (1827). See *Sämtliche Werke I/1 (Düsseldorfer Ausgabe)*, "Buch der Lieder" Text, ed. Pierre Grappin

(Hamburg: Hoffmann und Campe, 1957), p. 163.

84 These words come from the afterword to Hearn's translation *Clarimonde* (New York, NY: Brentano's, 1899), p. 79. The translator appends a poem by Gautier to this volume, and adds a note on that. But his assessment is the same elsewhere. In the preface to a larger selection, *One of Cleopatra's Nights and Other Fantastic Romances* (New York, NY: R. Worthington, 1882), Hearn notes their 'peculiar beauty', p. v.

85 In fact, Waddell may have taken this story from Yone Noguchi since, like him, she gets the names the wrong way round. This story, and that of Oto-Tachibana, are related in his book *The Spirit of Japanese Poetry* (London: John Murray, 1914), pp. 75–84. The order of the names has been corrected here. Waddell quotes two poems from this book in 'The Hyacinth Fields', and it is mentioned in her letters.

86 *Kaidan Botan-dōrō* [Peony Lantern Ghost Story] by San'yūtei Enchō. 'San'yūtei Enchō' was the stage name of Izubuchi Jirokichi (1839–1900), a well-known contemporary *rakugo* performer, some of whose performances were transcribed and made into books. His version of the *Botan-dōrō* was published in 1884. (The tale was originally Chinese, but had been domesticated long before this.) It was also turned into a Kabuki play, which in turn inspired Hearn's recounting of the story.

87 *Troilus and Cressida*, Scene III, Act ii. See *The Complete Works of Shakespeare* ed. Peter Alexander (London: Collins, 1951), pp. 805–7.

88 Review of Arthur Waley, *Japanese Poetry: 'The Uta'* by (Oxford: The Clarendon Press, 1920), in the *Nation*, 13 March 1920. See Appendix for the full review.

89 *Bridge Head* was first performed in Dublin in 1934 and later in London, in 1939, before being published there by Constable, the firm that Helen Waddell worked for. The play is about land redistribution in the Irish Free State after it became independent. The improbably named Japanese character, Inari Gosuki, has come to observe this on behalf of his government, and his ingenuous observations and enquiries form a comic foil to the action. In a sense Helen returned the compliment to her brother by seeing this play into print, since he had been largely responsible for the publication of her play about Japan, as she explains in a letter to Taylor on 7 August 1919: 'As a matter of fact, it was the Talbot Press who wrote to me about the play – their "reader" had got it from my brother, the playwright, in manuscript.'

90 Poem XL in *A Shropshire Lad* (1896). See *The Collected Poems of A.E. Houseman* (London: Jonathan Cape, 1948; first published 1939), p, 58.

91 George Buchanan, *Morning Papers* (London: Gaberbocchus, 1965), p. 46. This is the second volume of his autobiography and includes references to Helen Waddell. Buchanan knew her in London at the time she was writing *Peter Abelard*, which she would read aloud to him, chapter by chapter, as it progressed. His first books were published by Constable, partly with her assistance.

92 See Corrigan, *Helen Waddell*, p. 201.

93 Ibid., p. 283. The letter seems to be undated. The word 'chobo' which occurs in it was the Waddell family word for lavatory. It probably derives from *chōzuba*, an antiquated word for this in Japanese.

94 Quoted in Helen Waddell, *Poetry in the Dark Ages* (Glasgow: Glasgow University, 1948), pp. 14–15. The translation is from the *Satyricon*, pt. 119. It has been collected, together with the Latin original, in *More Latin Lyrics: From Virgil to Milton* trans. Helen Waddell, ed. Felicitas Corrigan (London: Victor Gollancz, 1976), pp. 52–5. These lines are fom the opening section. For more detailed discussion, see Burleigh, 'The Early Writings of Helen Waddell on Japan', p. 76.

95 *Mediaeval Latin Lyrics* (London: Constable, 1948; first published 1929), pp. 328–30; *The*

Wandering Scholars (London: Constable, 1990; first published 1927), p. 88.

96 See the discussion of Evrard in Chapter III, and, especially, of Robert in Chapter VII, *Peter Abelard: A Novel* by Helen Waddell (London: Constable, 1992; first published 1933), pp. 13–15, 69–70.

97 See M.T. Clanchy, *Abelard: A Medieval Life* (Oxford: Blackwell, 1997), pp. 223, 262–3. There is something of it too in Waddell's virginal devotion to older men. See Corrigan, *Helen Waddell, passim*; also the note appended by the biographer to a new edition of *Lyrics from the Chinese* issued (by the Malvern Publishing Company) at Stanbrook in 1987.

98 Blackett, *The Mark of the Maker*, p. 219.

PART 1:

After Strange Gods:
Stories of Childhood

After Strange Gods

It was a fine morning, up among the hills. Billy and I sat on the verandah steps and fidgeted. Something was pricking inside us, and we longed to go on pilgrimages. We were tired of the village, now that the great heat had driven the rest of the missionaries from the brick houses of the Foreign Concession in Tokio, and sent them up here for a breath of mountain air. The place was full of them. We who had been here for a month of blessed loneliness and were soon to go back, scowled at the laden jinrickshas, and swung our bare brown legs from the verandah in defiance of 'Foreigners', – as we, Japs born and bred, were wont to call them – unfortunates who had come to the Land of the Lotus in their maturer years, and wore shiny boots and black stockings. We had known they were coming. The butcher had set up his shop the week before, and Kameyasan had sported a fresh stock of goods in that dim cool interior, which contained all things from scented tooth powder to tinned salmon. It was always a treat to go to Kameyasan's, especially if you had two sen to spend on chocolate boxes with Parisian ladies on the cover – incongruous enough in that remote Japanese village, though the incongruity did not strike us then. Besides, to reach him you had to go across the bridge that swayed deliriously when you were in the middle and Billy jumped on the other end. The stream came down from the mountains, and hurried underneath with a cluck and a gurgle that was cruel temptation to bare legs passing over it. But you mustn't paddle here, because there was a lot of broken delf, and you might cut your feet and get lockjaw; so ran the maternal orders in council. Doubtless there were many places down stream, apparently as seductive, yet Billy and I wondered for many a day why Sensei* laughed so whole-heartedly when we spent a whole morning laboriously clearing away every scrap of blue earthenware shining through the brown water and then dragged him down by way of Royal Commission on Public Safety. And again, that very afternoon when we came to him in wrath and grief to tell him that Mrs. Kameya had smashed the bowl in which she washed the rice upon that very spot. Sensei's ideas of humour were incomprehensible, but irresistible.

* Rabbi is the nearest equivalent (author's note).

But on this morning we had not two sen. We were tired of playing with Kate Lascelles, who lived in the big red bungalow facing ours. She had been doing lessons the night before, and had come to George Washington and Bunker's Hill, and she was Yankee enough to rub it in. So Billy went round the house, and brought our two sticks, the one with the snaky head he always kept for himself, and announced that we were going to do pilgrims, and to do it right you mustn't put on your sandals – this, though the paths were three inches deep in lava, the outward and visible sign that old Asamayama, twelve miles away, could do something more than light up the sky with a homely red flare every evening when darkness fell. I glanced doubtfully down at my bare feet, and my toes wiggled anxiously, deprecatingly.

'That's you!' said Billy scornfully – 'and you practising Early Christian Martyrs at home!'

That taunt settled it. I had reason to remember the morning when Billy had found me stepping painfully along the path where they threw the cinders, with tender, bare soles, and in an evil hour had wiled me into explanation.

So we set out, Billy and I, along the Pilgrim's Way, the road that the Daimyo used to travel in the bad old days, marching down with his samurai knights to do homage to his feudal lord in ancient Yedo. It winds to this day among the hills, high on the slopes of them, in fine disdain of the toy train down in the hollows, that puffs and pants through six hours and twenty-six tunnels once a day from Tokio. The pilgrims travel it too – or used to – to the shrine away among the further hills, beyond even Karuizawa, the Temple of the Togi Pass, from which on a clear day you may see the Sacred Mountain itself. This was the road which we chose that day for pilgrimage; and – what does not happen to all pilgrims – this was the road that brought us before the Ancient Gods.

It happened on this wise. It was very hot. The sunlight filled the valley with an intense yellow radiance, even – so someone said – as water fills a jug. We had long passed the little wooden church where the missionaries had met that day for conference. The door was open as we went by, and we caught a glimpse of Sensei's grey head bowed at the reading desk, and a hush as if someone were praying, although we heard no voice. But it was Strange Gods we sought that day, and we went our pagan way, Billy breaking as he went into the dreary little wailing chant that you hear so often on the Pilgrim Roads. He had the artistic sense, Billy – always.

But the chant soon died away. The road had been climbing up for the last half mile; so had the sun. Its rays were nearly vertical: away before us stretched the Pilgrim's Way, an interminable white line, steadily rising as it went, unshaded, uncompromising. But on either side of it the pine woods rose, very stately, very shadowy, and we knew that in their depths the sunlight softened to a mellow haze. Temptation tugged at our hearts; we went a little slower; and at the turn of the road the crisis came. For to our left there fell away a little path among the bracken, a brown earthen path, with green moss on it, and roots of trees rising here and there to make the descent easier. And it ran, not straight and masterful, like the Pilgrim's Way, but winding and suggestive, disappearing finally into we knew not what depths of green enchantment. We stopped by a kind of mutual consent. Even Billy was wavering. But the white road called him, challenged him, rather. Once again he had set his face to it, had all but stirred, when the woods flung their last snare. There came a wistful rustle among the pine branches; they leaned towards us, entreatingly; and from the depths of them came that strange small wind, the breath of the hushed and silent places, the pungent fragrance of warm brown earth and fallen pines.

It had been churlish to refuse such invitation. Without one backward glance we plunged into that sunset way. To this day I can feel the grateful touch of moist earth on wayworn pilgrim feet, the coolness and silence that drew us, farther and farther, into sunlit depths of peace. On and on we went; then suddenly, came on signs of habitation, not of men, but of gods. Arching the pathway stood an old 'tori', the quaint entrance gate of single uprights and curving crossbeam, that marked the spot we stood on as holy ground. We stopped, uncertain. We had no great acquaintance with what might lie beyond. True, we had gone last summer with Sensei to the great temple at Shiba, where the Shoguns lie buried; and the old clean-shaven, soft-spoken priest had been very gracious with the children, and had given us sweet cakes from before the very altar, whereat Sensei had smiled a little and murmured something in Greek, but had not hindered us. And then he had talked a long while with the old man, and finally been taken by him into the great dim library, where few foreigners entered, while we fed the doves in the sunny courtyard with crumbs of the sacred bread. What if there were like entertainment beyond these silent sentinel 'tori' – kindly soft-voiced priests, and cake – ay, truly, cake: welcome, for the sun was high, and dinner-time was surely near. So with stout heart, and hoping all things, we pushed forward.

But there was something eerie about the place. The good brown earth had given way to broad flag-stones, but green moss grew on them, grass even had pushed its way between them. The pines had yielded to the giant cryptomeria which grows around all sacred places in Japan, and the shadows were blue, instead of golden brown. And as we went the trees seemed to grow taller and the shadows deeper. High above head we could see the flecks of blue sky, but the sunlight only lay in little splashes, like yellow stains on the old, untrodden stone. It was lonelier far than the empty spaces of the wood, lonely with that awful desolation that comes upon a place where men have once been, and now are not. But still we pushed on, with that fatalism which is in all children, until the pathway took a steep descent down many broken steps. At its foot there lay a hollow, steeped in sunlight and in stillness, and in the midst of it, a ruined shrine. It did not need the stone laver empty of water, the broken stone lanterns raised to the memory of untended dead, the massive crumbling roof, to tell us that worshipper and priest had long departed. There was an emptiness upon the place. It ached with silentness. And for crown of desolation, the rice-bowl, empty, still stood upon the altar steps, as if the god himself had stooped to seek an alms.

There was a sudden movement; Billy had stirred beside me. It was only to lift his hand and take off his helmet, but slight as it was, the spell had been broken, and we moved forward; quickly, for the sunlight was grateful after the sombre darkness. The fear of the place was still upon us, but so was our curiosity, and we were at the very steps of the shrine when I started back with a sudden cry. For the gods had not been left without a protector. There on the warm stone lay basking their self-constituted guardian, a sleeping snake. There was one moment of horrified recoil, then with the quick relief of physical effort after supernatural terror, Billy sprang forward with the joy of battle in his eye, and struck the creature with his pilgrim staff. It was a harmless one, doubtless; perhaps, like all else in that desolate spot, it was very old. For in a few seconds the thing was done, the swift thudding of the stick had ceased, and Billy stood beside me panting, gazing at the long dead line, its head battered into shapelessness, quiet on the sunny stone. And once again the silence came down upon us, gripped us as surely as an invisible hand. The dark trees seemed to close around the sunbathed hollow in which we stood, guilty, and trapped. There was something sinister in the very glare of the sunlight. And there before us lay the snake – dead, in that place of death.

I caught Billy by the sleeve, glancing furtively at the shrine, vengeful in its empty darkness. 'Billy,...do you think it belonged to...Them?'

Was it our fancy, or did something indeed stir and take shape within the sombre void? We did not wait to see. Breathless, frenzied, we dashed up the ruined steps; the darkness of the cryptomeria fell upon us like a chilly dew; our bare feet pattered wildly among the mossy flags. On we fled, reckless with terror, heedless of the scorching blaze on the white road. On we fled in the grip of that mad terror, our hearts beating against our ribs, and our breath coming in gasps, down a road familiar enough, yet strange and fearful to our awakened nerves. And still the accusing silence seemed to pursue us, till, with what relief no man knows, there fell upon our ears the sound of singing. Fear had indeed given us wings. We were already at the little church, and never was mediaeval fugitive in as sore need of sanctuary.

'God is our refuge and our strength' – the old Scottish psalm tune rose and fell, with a sudden blessed assurance of strong protection in its venerable cadences. The two small pagans in the church porch sank on the steps with the sob of a vast relief.

'God in the midst of her doth dwell', again swelled out to us. We listened, enveloped in a great peace. Gradually the familiar everyday world closed again around us, the familiar voices distinguishing themselves to our accustomed ears, with a certain gracious sense of security. And once again the battle psalm of the Covenant did its work. For when I looked up, Billy was on his feet.

'I'm not going to run any more,' he announced with a magnificent bravado, – 'it's far too hot for races.' I looked at him, speechless with admiration, and we trudged home, in a great and comforting silence.

And so curious a thing is human nature, that when the familiar red bungalow came in sight, and on the opposite verandah a small American face with a tight pigtail over one shoulder, Billy's step quickened.

'Kate! Kate! We've killed a – guess – a SNAKE!'

Kate was upon us like a flash. 'Where is it?' she demanded, with a fine practical scepticism.

'We didn't bring it with us', said Billy grandly, 'it was too big'.

'Then you may just take me to it after dinner', said Kate conclusively.

I looked at Billy furtively, just in time to catch the almost imperceptible shudder that passed over him. We turned and looked back. He saw it too, as well as I, the silent sun-steeped hollow with its black belt of trees, the sinister empty shrine, the dead snake lying like a stain on the warm stone … No, we would not go back.

'You – your mother wouldn't let you go so far!' said Billy, triumphantly, jeeringly. He had a singular control of his emotions, even from his youth.

Kate's face fell. It is hard to be the only daughter of your mother, and she a widow.

'Well, show me the stick you killed it with, any way,' she said, in the manner of one who seeks matter of offense.

I had not looked at it since, and I shrank a little. For the snaky head seemed still more life-like in its sinister reptile outline; the knot that we called the eye watched us with a venomous intentness, and on the flat head of it there was a dull blue stain.

Billy shivered – again that imperceptible shiver – and plunged the head of it with a sudden jerk into the bowl of water where Kate had been swimming gold-fishes. To our excited imagination, the water turned a curious ugly blue.

'Ugh!' said Kate. Then with an exquisite feminine volte-face – 'Ah Billy, you might let me have it!'

Billy visibly wavered. But the boy in him came uppermost, trampled on both woman and superstition.

'Look here, Kate, don't – don't ask me for it till I get showing it to those Spencer chaps down in Tokio.'

It was an argument that appealed to Kate; but being a woman, she looked at him, none the less, over her shoulder, poutingly. And Billy wavered, was on the verge of surrender, when the gods sent a diversion. For our old Jap servant appeared on the opposite verandah. 'Taberu yurushi, Biri-san' (Dinner, Master Billy!) and we fled to satisfy what is after all the oldest of all deities.

But on the long train journey down to Tokio, a week later, I noticed Billy sitting silent and distrait by the open window, visibly regretting. I looked, and his hands were empty, though now and then they made as though to close around a beloved object.

'Billy – what have you done with that stick?' I asked impetuously.

'Mind your own business', said Billy morosely.

And I knew.

Notes

'go on pilgrimages': Bands of Buddhist pilgrims frequently passed through Karuizawa during the summer at that time.

'the Foreign Concession in Tokio': See the Introduction, p. 7.

'jinrickshas': Waddell's spelling hovers between the original Japanese *jinrikisha* (lit. 'man-power-vehicle') and the later modified English word 'rickshaw'. This form of transport was invented in Japan at the beginning of the Meiji period.

'Kameyasan [Kameya-*san*]': Kameya was the shop owner's name. In her diary entry for 4 July 1898, Margaret notes: 'Cleared up, and went to Kameya. Bought 6 sen of chocolate.' The next day she says: 'Went to Kameya's and bought 12 sen of chocolate, also beancakes.' But three days later, on 8 July, she notes: 'Kameya's shop broken into last night. 100 yen stolen.'

'two sen [*sen*]': One hundred *sen* equalled one *yen*, which was the largest monetary unit. There were three even smaller units than *sen*, but these were not much used. Margaret supplies an idea of the value when she describes the family's financial difficulties on 27 July 1898: 'How much money have I? About 24 sen (6 pence). Not much.' But much more than today, of course.

'Sensei [*sensei*]': A term of respect widely used for teachers, or anyone in a senior position; its approximate meaning is 'one who goes before'.

'Kate Lascelles': Kate Large, Helen's best friend, who frequently appears in Margaret's diary. See the Introduction, p. 20.

'you mustn't put on your sandals': Japanese pilgrims are not barefooted, so Waddell seems to be thinking of other, perhaps Christian, pilgrims. In her diary entry for 17 May 1900, Margaret observes: 'Helen has bare feet.' But this was in the garden of their house in Tokyo, and it seems unlikely that the children would have made a long walk through the country in this condition.

'Asamayama [Asama-*yama*]': Mount Asama is an active volcano whose slopes are covered with lava cinders, on the border of Gunma and Nagano prefectures.

'the road that the Daimyo used to travel': The *daimyō* and their relatives were required to spend a certain amount of time in the capital during the Edo period (1603–1867) so that the shogun could control them. The road referred to is the Nakasendō, the mountain route connecting Tokyo and Kyoto, as the Tokaidō connected them along the coast. The Nakasendō had sixty-nine 'stations', to the Tokaidō's fifty-three. Karuizawa was one of these stopping-places.

'the toy train … six hours and twenty-six tunnels': Margaret records, on 22 June 1898: 'Going to Karuizawa. Rose at about 3 a.m. Dark. Paid [servant?]. Good bye to wee tooto's [pet dove]. Got card from O Yuki san [friend]. It was fine day. Started for station. Sun getting up. Dark clouds. Met Mrs. Davidson, More [Mrs Moore] and Mr. Moore. Had a long time, 6 hours in train. First part country flat, full of rice-fields. At Takezaki [Takasaki] changed train. Sun out a little. Varied country fields and hills. Birds singing. Little German engine (Dibsch) backed us up the hills. Twenty-six tunnels, 6 and 26 longest. Reached Karuizawa. One mile to Mrs. D. house. Air cool and refreshing. Surrounded by mountains. Big Moors all around. Mrs. D. house has two verandas covered with Wisteria. Helped to tidy house.' At that time the train had only recently been extended to Karuizawa.

'Temple of the Togi Pass': 'Togi [*Tōge*] Pass' is tautological, since *tōge* means 'pass'. There are several mountain passes in the area, but the one referred to here is probably Usui Tōge, which was crowned by 'a poor grey village, with a temple to keep watch over the pilgrims who pass through it in the summer-time', according to Mary Crawford Fraser, *A Diplomat's Wife in Japan: Letters from Home to Home* (London: Hutchinson, 1900), p. 384.

'the Sacred Mountain': Mount Fuji, which was an important site of pilgrimage and veneration.

'"tori" [*torii*]': This usually indicates the entrance to a Shinto shrine, rather than a Buddhist temple, though it can be placed before either. The buildings are sometimes adjacent and the division is not always clear or absolute. But here, from the mention of 'gods', it seems to be a shrine.

'the great temple at Shiba': There was originally a large park at Shiba, in south-western Tokyo. This place had been chosen as the burial ground for some of the shoguns, and contained several important mausoleums, as well as Zōjōji, the chief temple of one Buddhist sect. The buildings were evidently remarkable for their decorations, but were mostly destroyed in the air raids of World War II, though the main building of the temple had been destroyed earlier by fire. The buildings that stand on the site today are reconstructions. There was also a colourful and much visited market or bazaar (*kankōba*), notable for its varied goods and novel entertainments.

'seek an alms': This is a Buddhist, not a Shinto, practice.

'"Taberu yurushi, Biri san."': Probably intended to be *'Tabete yoroshii, Birii-san'* (lit. 'Eating is fine, Master Billy'), though as a form of address *san* is most commonly employed for adults, while *chan* is more usual for children.

Kwannon of the Single Grace

Up through the pines came the small tinkling of a bell. I stopped trickling warm white sand through my fingers and listened. For a long hour the trees had been still; the world slept in the heat, and the sea came and went very softly on the sand. There was a cicada on the branch above our heads: he was preternaturally small and very shrill, but even he had slept from sheer exhaustion. Now the tinkling disturbed him, and he wakened and was very vehement. I laughed at him, but Billy only shut his eyes tighter, and his lips moved faster. He was praying for that white rabbit.

The tinkling came clearer, and now behind it one could hear a soft droning – 'Rokkon shojo, rokkon shojo, Oyama Kaisei.' Down on the road they were praying that their six senses might be pure, and the honourable-mountain-weather propitious. It is the Pilgrim's Chorus in Japan.

'Rokkon shojo, rokkon shojo' – 'Billy, it's the Fuji Pilgrims this time. Do stop, and come down to the tent.'

But Billy had his fingers in his ears. It was minutes before he took them out, opened his eyes and looked around him, blinking. He seemed a little dazed.

'I said I'd pray it a hundred times and I've done it. And I'm never going to pray for that white rabbit any more. I knew it would be no use anyway.' He plunged down the hill in a settled gloom.

'Rokkon shojo, rokkon…' The chanting abruptly stopped. This meant that the evangelist had come out of the tent and invited them in for tea. It is very hot in the Kamakura road, and when the evangelist would suggest that honourable throats parched must be, there would only be a slight demur against encumbering his august house with the impediment of their persons. The tent was just inside the shadow of the pines, away from the glitter of the sea, and the evangelist was a nice man, with blue spectacles and a thin pleasant voice. Sometimes he sang to the pilgrims while they drank his tea, and sometimes he preached a little. There were some very highly coloured prints of our Lord on the canvas. Sensei did not like them much, and never preached from them any time that the tinkling of the bells brought him down from the hill. But the Mission was not his Mission, and none of his business to criticise. It was really Miss Van Bilt's Mission. Miss Van Bilt's face was very red, like the Buddhist devil at the bottom of Billy's porridge bowl; she was very large, and she had irate gold-rimmed spectacles, and now and then she charged Kamakura and then the evangelist had the air of one temporarily submerged. She owned the bungalow on the hill, a shack of a place fastened down with iron rods lest the typhoons should lift it bodily, and when Sensei was ordered off from Tokio for two months, Miss Van Bilt swept him here. He did not want to go to Kamakura; he wanted to go to the hills; but your father never knew what was good for him; Miss Van Bilt knew that sea-bathing was the one thing. The heat was terrific; but, as Sensei said cheerfully, not really so very much worse than it had been in Tokio. And there was always shadow under the pines, and a small wind stirred in them after sunset, and all night long the thunder of the Pacific broke on the beach. Also, there were no foreigners nearer than Kamakura beyond the shoulder of the hill, and not another house in all the pine-clad bay, and only pilgrims passing on the road. Pilgrims had a fascination for our father, as for us. We very often found him lounging at the tent door, and talking in his drifting fashion, what he called 'brushing up his colloquial'. He was rather proud of his colloquial.

He was standing there now; we could see his white ducks gleaming through the pines as we straggled down the hill. There seemed to be many pilgrims, and they looked as if they had come far. Billy's gloom lightened perceptibly. After all, the world is full of a number of things, though empty

Pilgrims on the road.

of rabbits, white rabbits, with pink noses that twitch. We were rather tired of Kamakura pilgrims; these were Fujisan, the great white mountain that we had seen one clear morning rising on an empty sky-line, and thought we had dreamed it. These were in white, too, the *kimono* tucked into the girdle, and the name of the pilgrim club in big black characters on their backs, and on the great white bason hats. That must be the leader that Sensei was talking to; he knew the roads, and what shrines were worth stopping at, and which of the priests would let you see the Kwannon for least cash, and which of the inn keepers were honest. He was very brown, this man, and Sensei seemed to be liking him. There was also an O Basan, the only woman of the party, and a small grand-daughter to wait on her. O Basan was very old. Also she was very hideous. Her eyebrows were shaved off, and her teeth blackened, just like our old nurse down in Tokio. We used to think it was to save her from ever having to brush her teeth any more, but she said it was done when she married, so that no other man would find her good to look upon. And when I asked her if her husband would not like to find her good to look upon, she said he never thought of that. All the same she had a nice face, and so had this O Basan. It went into funny creases when she laughed, and she did that very often. She did it first when I asked her if she was climbing Fujisan.

She was staying in Kamakura, was O Basan. Did I not know, Fujisan was not for women to climb; it was too holy for that. Did I not know that even the sand that the Pilgrims carried on their sandals from the lower roads went sliding down the mountain at night? One could hear it if one lay awake. Shinzo yonder – her unintelligent son who now the honourable foreigner inconveniencing was – had heard it often. Shinzo was climbing Fujisan. He would acquire merit. Shinzo had acquired much merit. All the village had subscribed this time, and chosen the pilgrims, and they were all acquiring much merit, and the village would divide it up when they got home. But O Basan would wait in Kamakura till they came down again. No, it was not the great Daibutsu that she had come to pray to, it was Kwannon, Kwannon the Hundred-armed, Kwannon the Pitiful. Only for him yonder she would not have come. She would stay in Kamakura with her mother's brother's son. He was Cooksan at the big hotel where the foreigners stay, and wore a white hat. He was married and had three sons – not like Shinzo.

Was Shinzo not married? To be sure Shinzo was married. But Shinzo was a fool. Although he was her eldest son, and she owed him the Third Obedience. It was really because of the folly of Shinzo that O Basan had come so far. Shinzo was married, but Shinzo had no son.

Girls? To be sure there were girls. Five girls. But what were girls? I looked round furtively for Billy, but he was listening with intent to Shinzo and Sensei. So much the better. Thanks to the folly of Shinzo, there would be no one to set incense-sticks before the Butsu-dan, and no one to worship the ancestors, O Jisan, nor O Basan, nor yet Shinzo himself, when in time he too became an ancestor. Girls! They would marry husbands, and then they would have their husbands' ancestors to worship. Girls! And O Basan sharply summoned the small and wonderfully cheerful grand-daughter to fill her pipe. The small grand-daughter was having the time of her life, and the problem of the derelict ancestors had not yet begun to weigh upon her.

Was it the fault of Shinzo? To be sure it was the fault of Shinzo. He could have divorced his wife – long ago he could have divorced his wife – for much less than this, and married a new one. He might have had ten sons by this time. But Shinzo was a fool. And now they were coming to pray to Kwannon. Kwannon was a woman herself, and so much better for this sort of thing than Buddha. Kwannon understood. It was true that they had come many times to pray to Kwannon, but this time – did I not know? – Kwannon has a name, Hito Koto Kwannon, and when one prays to her by that name, one gets whatever one has asked. But one may never pray to her by that name again. And Shinzo was going to use his prayer. It might so easily have been done otherwise. This was the folly of Shinzo. One never knew when one might need it. But Shinzo was obstinate, obstinate as a pack horse. To be sure O Tsuyusan was good enough. She did talk much. O Basan did not like a woman who talked. Would it be permitted a disreputable old woman to ask another cup of the August's honourable tea?

The evangelist's little wife brought the cup, serving on her knees. The baby on her back looked on O Basan with beady eyes. O Basan had a fresh text. Now was my chance to find why Billy was listening so intently. He had even forgotten to drink his tea. Usually Billy emptied the cup in great swoops, breathing heavily. This is etiquette in Japan, to make noises of gratification as one eats; viewed from the East Billy's table manners were perfect.

Shinzo was squatting on his heels, and smoking leisurely. 'There was a foreigner, Honourable One, last year, when the mountain was open, but she said not as you. She was very great,' he went on retrospectively, 'and there were yellow rims to her eyes...like an owl's.'

Sensei nodded gravely.

'She said when one prayed at the shrines, there was not any one to hear, or if there were, it was an 'oni'. She said that to pray to Kwannon and Buddha was to pray to devils. It is not a true word, Sensei?'

'It is not a true word.'

'But, Honourable One, is it true that Kwannon and the Buddha do not hear?'

For a while my father said nothing. 'See you, O Shinzo,' he began at last, 'it is like this. To me it is like this. Suppose that a beggar came to the Imperial Palace at Tokio, to the Outer Moat – when the daimyos were passing in; and the daimyos did not hear. But the Emperor', Sensei lifted his sunhelmet, and Shinzo bowed himself, 'the Emperor himself was passing and heard, and gave: and the beggar did not see him.'

Shinzo's face had kindled; it fell as suddenly. 'And all this way…and the many shrines…and the dust…and the fees to the priests…and the sore feet at night – Sensei, is it all for naught?'

'Hardly for naught', said my father slowly, 'since Joh Te* saw it, and knew'.

'Then, Honourable One, will Joh Te give me my son?'

My father hesitated. Billy was watching him, defiantly, and now he dug an impatient toe in the sand. Shinzo's eye fell upon him. There is nothing in the world so kind as the face of a Japanese when he looks at a child.

'Is the Bochan yours, Honourable One?'

'Aye, and seven like him. This is the least of them, Shinzo.'

'Think you, Honourable One', Shinzo's voice was very eager, 'that if I worshipped Joh Te, even as you worship him, He would give me a son?'

My father looked miserably out to sea.

'I could not promise, Shinzo. One is never sure.'

The light died out of Shinzo's eyes. Then suddenly he remembered. 'Ay, but Honourable One', he cried triumphantly, 'I am sure. For hearken, you know of Hito Koto Kwannon, Kwannon of the Single Grace? All my life I have kept that prayer. All my life. But to-night we go, O Basan yonder and I, and I shall pray to Kwannon by her great name that she give O Tsuyusan to bear a son. And Kwannon cannot refuse.'

He ended on a wistful note. Almost he appealed for confirmation; but my father had no words. In the silence O Basan's crackled treble shrilled from the tent.

'It was but last summer, I tell you, and Iijima was out of himself by reason of his brother Sassosan. For Sasso ate even like unto a silk worm and did naught, and continually he returned to Iijima and tormented him. And Iijima went one night and prayed to Kwannon by her great name that he might be set free, and but the next night Sassosan came home, having drunk much saké, and went being thirsty to draw water from the well, and in pulling up the bucket was drowned. And moreover, it was not even Iijima's well, for then would Sasso have haunted the house of Iijima, but the well of a neighbour against whom there was no injury. Wherefore there is no one to be distressed. Truly it is a prayer of efficacy. Did I not say that Shinzo was a fool?'

Shinzo rose to his feet a little wearily. Doubtless he has heard it many times. Outside the tent the shadows of the pines were stretching on the road.

*The Heavenly Emperor (author's note).

'O Basan', he called, 'it is still a *ri* to Kamakura. Honourable One, will you be here when we return again?'

'It is my grief', said my father, 'but I fear not. See', he had been scribbling on a piece of paper, 'will you send me this from Sakai – if Joh Te sends a son?'

It was received with many salutations. Leave taking is a lengthy business in the East, but at last it was over, the final *ojigi* had been performed, and my father had bowed many times as horizontal as a European back permits.

'Rokkon shojo' – Shinzo struck up the chant. Off they swung in long file, and one by one the blackness of the pines swallowed them up.

My father stood a long time looking after them; so did Billy. But for the shadow on Sensei's face there was an uncanny gleam about Billy, a curious exaltation. It boded ill.

It was very hot when I awakened that night; too hot to sleep again. The mosquito net smelt old and dusty: one mosquito had got inside and sang unceasingly. It was like the sinister night when we had brought home a bowlful of crabs and left them on the verandah, and roused in the middle of the night with the noise of small and stealthy goings somewhere in the dark; it was not till morning that we found it was crabs who had gone in dreadful procession round and round our beds. I wanted to stretch my arms under the pillow for coolness, and did not dare, lest a centipede should cling to my finger. This was Billy's peculiar horror, and quite conceivable, for the 'futons' were not more than three inches above the floor. There was a centipede in the tent yesterday; a black one, with orange rings. I saw it every time I shut my eyes. Altogether it was a relief when Billy's voice said cautiously, 'Are you awake?'

Billy's usual way of finding out was to loosen your mosquito net, and let it collapse on top of you. His courtesy made me anxious. Then he came under the net. He was dressed.

'I'm going to Kamakura', he said soberly, 'I wish you'd come along.'

I did not ask what for. I think I had known ever since I saw him watching the pilgrims disappear into the pines.

'Don't care whether it's right or not', he went on heavily. 'But I'm going to have that rabbit. And he said you never could be sure. And Shinzo said he was sure.'

There was no way out. 'They'll hear you opening the shutters,' I said weakly; but already I was on the floor, and Billy tugging at the 'earthquake door'. It is closed with staples and a wooden bar, and one usually has it open by the time the earthquake is over. By the time Billy had it open, I was dressed.

We stood at the doorway and looked out. The world was black and silver. Round the moon was a blaze of light, but the rest of the sky was so blue that it was black. The bay was silver with a fringe of foam, and from it the pineclad hills rose steep and black. The toad who lived under the verandah sat in the moonlight on the stone step, and looked at the sea. His back was wrinkled; he was very old, and his mouth was very wise.

'If you're afraid', said Billy at last, 'you needn't come'.

Was I afraid? Down at the edge of the sea twinkled a little red light, the only thing that was not black and silver in all the world. The tide was full, and it swayed with it uncertainly. What could any one be doing there? I remembered with a chill. To-night was the feast of the Bon: all day the spirits of the dead had been feasted in their old familiar homes, and with the dark they must put out to sea again in their frail straw ships, with food and incense and lanterns to light them to the underworld. This spirit had come down to the little river under the pines, and now had reached the sea, so much later than those luckier spirits whose ships had put off from the very verge. And now belated, it seemed still clinging to the warm shore. It was halting, reluctant, very wistful. Would it, could it, break away and come up the sands, and I waiting for Billy in the house alone? Better the road with its black pools of shadow. The fear of it had left me, but of that forlorn red light down on the shore I was horribly afraid. Another moment, and the smell of dust was in our nostrils, the strange pungent smell that comes when the dew has fallen, and our feet were padding softly along the silver road.

The Great Buddha.

It was half an hour before we halted in the shadow of a huge *tori*. It was not Kwannon's temple; that was still to come; it was Buddha himself who dwelt within. With a sudden swerve Billy led the way under the great gate.

Once there was a temple, but seven hundred years ago a tidal wave came in and swept it out to sea. They built it again and it [stood] another hundred, and again the sea came back for it, and Buddha was left alone. Now the giant cryptomeria grows round him, trees that are very old; but Buddha is older still. He sat in the clear space inside the belt of pines, and towered above us very black and very great; and the moon looked down on him and on us. He did not see us; we were hidden in the shadow at his feet.

With whatever vague impulse Billy had turned in, he made no sign. We had gone a little way along the road before he spoke. 'I didn't tell him', he said tonelessly. 'Someway…I don't think he'd care much about rabbits.' One felt dimly that it was true. After all, O Basan was right. Kwannon was better for this sort of thing.

Kwannon's temple has never been swept away. Through the gateway glimmered countless steps among the pines; the priest's houses were thick around her court, but they were silent with the heavy silence of sleep. Under the black sweep of her great temple roof we paused; somewhere behind the grating the Goddess of Mercy stretched out her kindly arms: a half burned incense stick sent up a faint spiral of blue smoke into the moon-steeped air.

Billy knelt, clapping his hands together softly. Twice he tried to speak, but the silence caught at his throat. 'Hito Koto Kwannon,' he began; then the memory of Sunday morning in the little church at Shiba came upon him, and he went on fluently in Japanese. 'Humbly we beseech Thee' – and he had caught the very cadences of Mr. Wada's voice in the opening prayer, 'humbly we beseech Thee that Thou wilt vouchsafe unto us' – the rapid utterance stopped. I opened my eyes and looked. Billy was staring at the shrine, his mouth open, his eyes wide and blank. There was a moment of terrible silence. Then he turned to me.

'I've forgotten', he choked, 'I've forgotten the Japanese for white rabbit'.

The minutes slipped past us, one by one. The silence in the courtyard gathered round us; it came nearer and nearer. And still we stood, straining in a sore dumb agony. With a sudden jerk, Billy turned and faced the shrine, his head held high.

'A WHITE RABBIT,' he finished in English, very slowly and authoritatively, as one speaks to a foreigner, 'A WHITE RABBIT.'

There was not any sound within the shrine. After all, Kwannon does not always work by miracle. Tomorrow it would come. The Kurumaya-san would bring it from the station in a basket, nibbling cabbage leaves. And at least we had routed the silence in the courtyard. It closed in behind us and followed us far off as we went down the steps.

The tide was far out when we came from under the tunnel of the pines. The moon had set, but the road shone with a faint glimmering; somewhere in the bay a tiny red light tossed uncertainly, drifting farther and farther out. The toad still sat on the stone below the verandah. He saw us coming and his mouth was very wise.

There came no white rabbit. Possibly Kwannon, although a goddess, does not understand English. Nor did there come any letter from Sakai.

Notes

'tinkling of a bell': The pilgrims carried small bells attached to their belts, both as a call to prayer and, when it fell silent, as a reminder of the impermanence of life.

'"Rokkon shojo...Oyama Kaisei [*Rokkon shōjō...o-yama kaisei*]"': The translation of the pilgrims' chant given in the text is quite correct.

'Fuji Pilgrims': Pilgrim clubs were formed in every community, and selected members were chosen from the group to go on a pilgrimage with a leader who had some experience. From these representatives, mostly men, blessings accrued to the community as a whole. The route through Kamakura in the direction of Mount Fuji, visiting temples along the way, was an important one.

'the evangelist': The evangelist was a native Japanese assistant, a sort of John the Baptist figure, who acted as both a harbinger and an intermediary.

'Sensei [*sensei*]': The manuscript shows this was altered to 'My/our father', and then restored again. The last revision has been adopted, here and elsewhere.

'Miss Van Bilt': Kate M. Youngman; the description here seems to accord with the photograph of her in a biographical dictionary, except for the spectacles, which she may have taken off. See the Introduction, pp. 9, 18–20.

'the bungalow on the hill': Describing the family's arrival at Kamakura in 1897, Margaret notes in her diary, on 4 August: 'Papa hired two kurumas [rickshaws]. Thought the cart would never come (Sneg hired it) for our luggage. Drove two miles to our house. Rice fields on the way. Our house small and on a hill. Only two rooms.' This account seems to tally with the one in the story, where the 'shoulder of the hill' suggests itself as the original of the 'headland' that Helen later wrote about. The distance from the station that Margaret gives is not great enough for the house to be beyond a headland.

'Fujisan [Fuji-*san*]': Mount Fuji, which is visible across the bay from Kamakura; *san* is an alternative reading of *yama*, the character for 'mountain'. Most of the people who climbed Mount Fuji in the Meiji period were pilgrims. They stopped at ten 'stations' on the way to the summit, but women were not allowed to ascend beyond the eighth. Of course, all this has changed today.

'were in white': Traditionally pilgrims dressed in white. In addition to the clothes described, they also wore leggings and carried a staff.

'O Basan [*o-bā-san*]': Granny, or grandma; the *o* is honorific.

'eyebrows were shaved off': Clearly an anachronism. Shaving off the eyebrows, which were then painted higher on the forehead, was a custom of women (and men) in the medieval court. It was meant to enhance, not diminish, beauty.

'teeth blackened': This had been the custom for married women in the Edo period, as described, though it was dying out fast by the late nineteenth century.

'Daibutsu': Lit. 'Great Buddha'; this seated bronze figure of Amitabha, over 13 metres high and uncovered, dates from the thirteenth century. The reasons that it sits outdoors are given in the story. It is one of the most celebrated sights in all Japan, and has been many times described.

'Kwannon [Kannon]': The figure of Kannon has several different representations, including one with a thousand (not, as the story says, a hundred) arms, to show that she is ready to assist in every way. The number is a poetic exaggeration, and the statue itself would have only about forty.

'Cooksan [Cook-*san*]': The cook (lit. 'Mr Cook').

'Third Obedience': According to Confucianism, a woman owed obedience first to her father, then to her husband, and lastly to her son.

'Butsu-dan [*butsudan*]': A family or household Buddhist altar.

'O Jisan [*o-jī-san*]': Grandad, or grampa; the *o* is honorific.

'Hito Koto Kwannon': Lit. 'One Word Kannon'; the explanation is correct.

'O Tsuyusan [*o*-Tsuyu-*san*]': 'Tsuyu' is the woman's given name. It was common at this time to precede the given name of a girl or woman with an honorific *o*, which was intended to soften the sound of it, distinguish it from a man's name, and convey a feeling of intimacy.

'oni [*oni*]': The handwritten version has 'evil spirit' written after this in pencil; it means 'devil'.

'O Shinzo': Shinzō is a man's given name, but an honorific would not have been used before it. Perhaps the 'O' was intended as an apostrophe.

'daimyos [*daimyō*]': This word for the feudal lords has now entered English. Waddell's partly revised manuscript, a typed version with handwritten alterations, gives the word both with an 's' and without. This is still an uncertain matter, though Japanologists would not usually add one for the plural. The manuscript also reveals that a portion of dialogue was deleted from the difficult discussion between Waddell's father and the Buddhist pilgrim.

'Bochan [*botchan*]': A boy; the young master.

'Sassosan [Sasso-*san*]': While Iijima is an ordinary family name, 'Sasso' is improbable as a given name.

'*ri*': About two and a half miles; a league.

'*ojigi* [*o-jigi*]': A bow.

'"futons" [*futon*]': A pallet and a quilt, stuffed with cotton, laid out at night for sleeping; the word has now become familiar in English.

'feast of the Bon': The Bon or O-Bon festival in some ways resembles All Souls' Day in the Christian calendar. For Buddhists, it is believed to be the time when the spirits of dead ancestors return to this world. Graves are visited, traditionally with lanterns; food and prayers are offered; and the three-day festivities include communal dancing. When the time comes for the spirits to return to the other world, lanterns with candles are floated on rivers or launched on small boats into the sea to carry them back. The festival takes place from 13 to 15 July, or on the same days in August in some regions. It is popularly known in English as the Feast of Lanterns because of their extensive use.

'Kwannon's temple': This is clearly the Hase Kannon temple, which sits on a hill overlooking the sea about half a mile from the Great Buddha.

'Kurumaya-san [*kuruma-ya-san*]': A rickshaw-man. A *kuruma* is a wheeled vehicle, and hence another word for rickshaw.

The Doorkeeper of Buddha

Toads are not evil; they are only different. They are not even ugly. At least, the one Elizabeth knew best was not. There were many toads in the garden; one who lived by the rainwater barrel in a pleasant dampness; one who lived under the stone bridge across the pond of the goldfish; one who lived with a smell of rotting wood in the sluice beside the well. Besides these, others of less note who lived under the bamboo fence where the morning-glory trailed, who came out only when the rain fell swift and hard, beating down its frail red and white and purple, and flooding out their holes. When Elizabeth came into the sodden garden to smell the wetness, they hopped away, cumbrously, croaking to themselves very softly. But the Toad who lived under the verandah never hopped away. He was older than the other toads, and perhaps he was stiff, but Elizabeth could not tell. She had never seen him moving. He lived under the verandah where the earth is never wet; it is dry and white and flaky, with a smell that one forgets when one grows too tall to be at home under a roof two feet high – Elizabeth was eight, but she was small and thin. No one knew where his hole was. He had never been seen going or coming: he was squat and motionless, or else he was not. He sat beside the great half-hewn stone from which one stepped out of the garden into Sensei's room, the last outpost of the great house that zigzagged in single rooms and stretches of connecting verandahs across the garden. It was like him to choose the last verandah. One turned the corner sharply into a shadow of pines; at noon to come here was to find darkness. The rest of the garden lay in white, dry glare, and the flags scattered in uneven pathways through the grass were dangerous to bare feet; but here there was no grass, and the ground was damp and firm and cool. It was best after sunset; the little space between sunset and the dark, when the things that have been beaten all day by the strong shafts of heat take breath again. It was then the Toad came out, and sat, and looked before him. Elizabeth came out too, for there is a madness comes with the dewfall when one must dip and swerve with the swallows; the Japanese old women say the Spirit is in the heels. But always when it was spent she came and sat beside the Toad. Sweet violets grew beside the posts of the verandah, and Elizabeth smelt them in the dusk, and wondered if the Toad did too. She thought not. He saw and heard, but she did not think he felt, or cared to feel. Once, greatly daring, she put out one finger and touched him, very lightly. His back was rugged and hard and cold. He did not stir: he sat and looked before him. Elizabeth was ashamed and sorry. It was as though she had shouted in an empty church.

She never spoke to him, not even that day to apologise. She was intimate with the lizards, and talked to them all day long. But with him speech was a superfluous thing, an impertinence. And because she had divined it, she vaguely felt that he was not ill-pleased when she came to sit beside him. It was his impassivity that held her. It was a great thing to sit so very still. It was not ignorance, nor apathy; she knew that he saw her, heard her breathless coming, but always he had the same steady regard. He had a wide mouth like all frogs, but it had not their fatuous wisdom. There was something about him self-contained, remote, tolerant. Afterwards, when Elizabeth saw the great Daibutsu at Kamakura, she had a curious sense of the familiar: yet the stillness of the Toad was the more compelling. The massive countenance of the Buddha is the countenance of the man who has achieved indifference; the Toad had the unsought directness, the eternity of the symbol.

Elizabeth was not articulate, even to herself, about these things; she only felt; understanding, as children understand, by association. And so far there was nothing in the world of kin to the Toad. It was as though he was older than anything she knew. He sat in the twilight below the verandah as in the archway of a different world. Other things linked together. At sunset the bells in St. Andrew's Cathedral rang for evensong, and Elizabeth climbed the maple at the end of the garden, out of sight of verandah and roof, and leaned back against the trunk where one could see nothing but blue and the sharp delicate etching of the young leaves – there is nothing like young leaves outside Paradise – and lay there, listening for the first clear shattering note, breaking the yellow light of the afternoon like an oarblade dipping into bright water and rising with a scattering of drops. All things fresh and green belonged to the carillon. Even Mr. Whitford, who was the curate of St. Andrew's and who came to see Sensei, was fresh and clean and young, and Elizabeth admired him in the detached manner of childhood until one day he came upon her gardening, and she fled from him, being barefoot and dishevelled and self-conscious, and he gave chase and was insolent in capture. Elizabeth had just read 'Ivanhoe', and was temporarily Rebecca, and this was not the manner in which Rebecca received advances. That same evening he sealed his damnation. For passing the verandah he caught sight of the Toad where he sat in obscurity, and paused before him interestedly. Then he stooped and poked him with his stick. Elizabeth felt a curious sense of drying inwardly. The Toad sat and looked before him; looked at the white-trousered legs of the Church of England, into them and through them. Mr. Whitford laughed self-consciously, and said 'Funny old chap'. Afterwards Elizabeth forgave him; she reflected that it was to cover his embarrassment.

It was a little while after that Elizabeth found things to which the Toad belonged. It had been a sultry day; the darkness was feverish with malaria and quinine, and for once she slept brokenly. It roused her from a ragged snatch of dreaming, a strange boom that seemed to pour into the emptiness of the night and fill it with sound, dominant and mournful. She had never been awake to hear it before, but she knew it for the temple at Uyeno, five miles away across the sleeping streets, the great bronze bell that the priests of the night vigil strike at dawn. There was no repetition of it, like the swift hurrying ripple of the carillon. [It was as though the tides of silence rose all night, and broke, and ebbed into silence again.] There was a finality about the single stroke, the symbol One become audible, in sound that had an echo of the Infinite. Elizabeth lay and heard the quiet flowing back again, and, listening, remembered the Toad. This was the sound for which the Toad must wait. This was his world, that began with twilight and ended with the dawn. He sat on the threshold of it. His world, and not hers.

Notes

'The Doorkeeper of Buddha': This is the title under which it was published in the *Manchester Guardian*, but the handwritten version has 'The Keeper of the Door'. One sentence only that did not appear in the printed version has been restored in parentheses, because it seemed to add something to the description. Other small differences have been ignored. Notes for another version of the ending are scribbled sideways in the margin of the last page: 'And because sound almost became visible to her, it was as though she watched the closing of a great door. She had not seen beyond it – it was a place dark and rich and still. The dawn came in…' It continues for another sentence, but trails off and becomes illegible. This piece and the next form one manuscript.

'zigzagged in single rooms…': The appearance of the house may have given this impression, though it is unlikely to have consisted of all single rooms. See the Introduction, p. 14.

'Daibutsu': See the note for the previous story.

'St. Andrew's Cathedral': The name of the church dates from 1879, and it became a Cathedral in 1887. The name of the curate is unknown.

'Sensei [*sensei*]': See the earlier notes on this.

'temple at Uyeno [Ueno]': Kan'eiji in Ueno was once a great and important temple, but had been destroyed by fire during fighting in 1868, at the time of the Meiji Restoration, and was replaced by only a modest structure. The mausoleums for the shoguns adjacent to the temple continued to stand, but they too were destroyed when Tokyo was fire-bombed in 1945. Waddell must have been thinking of another temple, perhaps nearer to where the family lived.

In Things Evil

There are things one is afraid of with one's mind, and things one is afraid of with one's body. There are also things which one fears and loathes at once, but mercifully there are not many. Elizabeth knew the things she was afraid of with her mind. Not the lizards, who lived a hot darting life in the stones round the pond. Elizabeth loved them, especially the young ones, with the blue-veined transparent feet. Not the rats who romped over the wooden ceiling, nor the 'hebi', the house-snake, who reduced their population and exercised among them a benevolent despotism. But of centipedes she was terribly afraid; centipedes and a small black flat thing that scuttled out of her chair one night and rattled across the floor. Of one thing she was afraid with her body, albeit her mind despised it. Once, when Elizabeth was six, she watched her brother gardening and was conscious of an unfamiliar coldness on her feet. She looked down, and a red earthworm crawled up between her toes. For long enough it was one of the things that Elizabeth saw in the interval when one lets oneself slip down the steep places which end in sleep, and it roused her shrieking.

That was a terror sheerly physical: rather an aversion than a terror. But there are worse things than worms. Elizabeth had never seen them until the summer that she went to the hills, and she and Kate Lascelles played together on the verandah. It came along the verandah one day, three slim inches of it, barred with black and orange and green, a strange phosphorescent green. It hooped itself as it came, and the long body rippled through all its length, arching and straightening alternately. And it came as if it knew it was coming. It was the first time Elizabeth had known the physical sickness of fear. Kate Lascelles opened her eyes at her. Hairies? They were nice soft furry things. They wouldn't do you any harm. Elizabeth watched with a straining wordless horror while the high-pitched American voice assured her that there were heaps of those things, that Karuizawa was swarming with them, that the trellis over at Elizabeth's house was thick with them. Elizabeth sat under the trellis that night with the purple wisteria hanging from it like black grapes in the moonlight, and thought of those other things that lay under its leaves and hooped themselves along its stems. When she fell asleep she dreamed that she was under pine trees, in the pleasant yellow light that shines from fallen pine needles turned to golden brown. The branch nearest her hung low, and as she stooped to go under it something hooped itself along it; and another; and another. The ground began to move; there was a stir among the pine needles. It was alive with them, some smaller than the thing she had seen that morning, some greater; they were all moving, the same monstrous heaving motion at which her heart stood still. They were moving towards her; and she was bare foot. She turned to run, but they were all round her, only for the little patch of earth on which she stood. They were on it now. One of them had arched itself to climb on her foot when Elizabeth awoke. It was her first nightmare; it beat the path for all succeeding torment. All her life Elizabeth had thirsted for it: all the boys had had it, had bragged of clogged pursuit, and superincumbent horrors. Elizabeth had been somewhat aggrieved by her privation. But now that nightmare had come, she did not recognise it; it would have made life easier for her if she had. This was a torture unshared; she tried to tell it in the daylight, and something in her fled from it shrieking. It was too intimate a horror.

With the extraordinary perversity of childhood Elizabeth came to make pets of them. Kate and she kept them in chocolate boxes, with an arch cut in the sides – it was Elizabeth's idea, this refinement of terror – for the thrill at the sudden sight of the abhorred head, and the slow heaving of the gorgeous body through the narrow passage. Kate and she raced their pets against each other. Elizabeth had trained herself to a certain dreadful pride in them, a shuddering familiarity. She even captured and fed on vine-leaves one creature, the biggest even Kate had ever seen, of whom even Kate was a little afraid, breathing more freely when his magnificence was restored to his prison. It was the third day of his captivity: after the heartshaking precarious pleasures of the Derby, Elizabeth and Kate kept house. It was Kate who screamed and pointed. Elizabeth's eyes followed that quivering finger. The beauty had escaped. He was on her frock, climbing, with that strange deliberate relentless advance which Elizabeth had learned to fear most in the world. Looking down at him so near, he had grown bigger: she saw the points of crimson in the hideous head: with every swift loop he was nearing her face. The whole world reared and sank again in ghastly circles of green and orange: then mercifully went black.

It was when Elizabeth was ten that she saw the final symbol of the under-side of the world. She was astride of a wall, and over-balancing, fell into a bed of nettles. They were hospitable; they did not sting; it was not for that she grew afraid. The fall had stunned her a little, and the nettles grew deep, and for a while she lay still and looked up. She saw that they were very wonderful. They were slim and tall and curiously unreal: even in the broad sunlight they had an element of ghostliness, things to be seen at night with a half moon. Their high misty heads were infinitely wicked, infinitely graceful. There was a strange green twilight down among the stems. Elizabeth began to remember a stone of uncut jade that used to lie on Sensei's writing-table. For jade is the colour of evil spirits: there is no light in it: it is one of the colours that were not created; it belongs to the world that is older than twilight, older than the Toad. Elizabeth had fallen among the stems of things whose surface was the world she knew.

She sat up, a little dizzy. There was a leaf on the level with her eyes, very near her face. On it a brood of hairy caterpillars had been hatched that day. They were no longer than her little finger nail, and they writhed and swarmed…

Notes

'In Things Evil': This title is given immediately below 'The Keeper of the Door' on the handwritten manuscript that these two pieces form. This episode follows the previous one after a space, and breaks off uncompleted at the end.

'hebi [*hebi*]': Snake, as indicated. Most snakes in Japan are harmless.

'her brother gardening': The only mention of him here.

'Kate Lascelles': As before, Kate Large, Helen's best friend.

'Hairies?': This was evidently the children's name for these insects. In part of her diary entry for 4 April 1900, Margaret writes: 'Mother bought pansies daisies primroses, & marigolds. Planted them. Killed a lot of hairy mushis [insects]. Beautiful day.' Two weeks later, on 18 April, she adds: 'Fixed my garden at back. Hairys are horrid.' This was at the house in Tokyo.

'Sensei [*sensei*]': See earlier notes.

The White Iris

The sun had gone down behind Hanarisan, the Mount of Snakes. Of a sudden they knew that they had come a long way. They had never been so near the Mount of Snakes before: it had a bad name. But in the late afternoon light its slopes had been green and friendly, and the iris in the swamp at its foot had the rich life of gems. It was none of your common blue iris, that grew in clumps wherever it was wet enough down in the Tokio garden. Here were acres of it, crimson and glowing, with cool strong stems very agreeable to cut. The twins were in the swamp a long time. Then the sun dipped, and the crimson turned sluggish red, and the pools black and evil, and Hanarisan leaned over and threatened them. It was good to get out of his shadow into the dying light on the moors.

But the Karuizawa moors are wide. Hanarisan did not seem to be receding as quickly as he might: he heaved an ugly shoulder against a green-gold sky. A great way off the little dusty road slipped through the moors, white and tiny and remote. They were carrying the irises in sheaves, and it dragged at their shoulders and breathed on them a faint sickly breath of honey and bruised stems. There was grit in their sandals, and the sharp sword-grass tore at their bare legs as they dragged through it. It grew long and deep in the hollows, and they were many. The twins trudged up and down them doggedly, but they had ceased to talk. So with a final stumble, they came to the brim of one hollow, and stopped dead.

They had come upon a Japanese burying-place: a few grey stones, rough hewn and oblong, like steps to a temple where no one comes to worship, and sandalled feet have never worn them smooth. They lay scattered here and there, and they were few, half a dozen at most, but the sunset was on them, and on the short white-bleached grass, and in the midst the glory that had held them. It was a strange thing in that lonely place: a clump of white iris, straight and slim, the intense white radiance of its full-globed bloom shining distinct against the old grey stone and the glow on the dry grass. The twins stood motionless, not in fear: simply that the natural soul of beauty in them was for once satisfied.

The sun's rim dipped from the cloud that had hidden it, and something of the unearthliness faded. The twins stirred; they eyed with growing disfavour the tumbled heap of colour in each other's arms. Crimson? It was no crimson. It was terra cotta.

'You'd think it was the Engineering College in Tokio', said Billy disgustedly.

'It's worse.' Elizabeth's eyes widened at the horror of their own imagining. 'It's like the speckles on that dead little snake – the red one.'

'Ugh!' said Billy, and let his armful go. He gazed down the slope to where the iris shone incandescent.

'That's like the Campo Santo in Genoa', he said firmly.

'It's nicer', said Elizabeth. Elizabeth was six when she saw the Campo Santo, and then with tear-dimmed vision, because she wanted her dinner. What she did remember was the whiteness of the seeds in the great red slice of water melon that she devoured in the little black archway outside it.

'Cry baby', said Billy, but mechanically. His eyes were fixed on the immaculate splendour below him. He took a step.

'Billy, you can't', cried Elizabeth. '*It's stealing*!' Her deep little voice rose to its highest note on the *e*. But Billy was ahead in the hollow, and his knife was out. Three he cut, and scrambled back to her. 'One's for you', he said handsomely. 'You can carry it if you like.' It was held out to her, with Billy's famous smile. Elizabeth took it weakly. Only as they left the hollow, she stole a glance over her shoulder. The bottom of the hollow was already in shadow: above on the brink the fallen iris smouldered like a trampled fire. But before her Billy was already on the march, holding his iris solemnly before him. He carried it like a lamp.

Their last look that night was on its snowy splendour, rising like Fujisan from the old earthenware vase that was the basis of all their schemes of decoration. They had set it in the gap of the shutters that opened on the verandah, that the cool air from the moors might breathe upon it, and the clear-cut outline gleamed against the background of quiet sky. In a great self-satisfaction they fell asleep.

It was some time before Elizabeth started, broad awake. The moonlight, the intense, almost blinding whiteness of the Japanese full moon, lay in a broad bar across the floor. The house was very still. Elizabeth leaned over to see if there were any yellow cracks of light shining between the boards, to show that someone was awake as well as she. For Sanagi san's room was below theirs, and on hot nights when the twins could not sleep they took it in turns to lie prone on the floor and watch Sanagi san preparing his ill-smelling supper of rice and *daikon*, or reading himself drowsy by the light of the *andon*, his high paper lamp with the wick floating in an earthen saucer of oil. Night after night it put the twins to sleep as well as himself, the curious droning chant which proved that Sanagi san had once been lettered, perhaps even a *samurai*, though now descended to be Cooksan to a foreigner. Their father judged him to be a dishonoured *samurai*, for he had no sword. He had a great liking for Sanagi san. And even when Sanagi san got drunk, which was not seldom – the twins knew when it was going to happen, because he always came in to prayers the morning before, and Miss Van Bilt said it was a scandal to the Mission – he refused to get rid of him. So night after night Sanagi san had been [wont] to read himself asleep with the Tale of the Forty-Seven Ronin, who had kept their swords until they died upon them.

But to-night the room below was quiet and dark. It must be very late. If only the moon would not shine so bright: it kept one awake. What strange noises there were at night. Did the stairs talk to one another when they creaked like that? Was it the stairs that had creaked? Was it not on the verandah? It would be lonely on the moors to-night. They would be very wide and very bare and very quiet. What made it so close? And what was that faint smell? The room was full of it. It was like honey, only there wasn't any honey. It was the white iris. Elizabeth turned and looked.

She had known all the time that it was there. It was because it was there that she had looked to see if Cooksan's *andon* were burning. It was not that she was afraid. There was not anything to be afraid of. But the smell was very heavy. That must be what was keeping her awake. If she put it out on the verandah it might clear the room. She would see the moors if she went on the verandah. They would be very quiet. One would be able to see very far off. One would almost see the hollow... After all, it was hardly worth while getting out of bed.

Was that a bird that was crying out on the moors? Why would it not go to sleep? Was it true what Sanagi san had said, that it was a lost soul that cried in the bird? Were any of the people under those grey stones lost souls? Would they be on the moors at night? Would they see some of their white iris had been cut? Did it belong to them? Ah but it smelt heavy, and how white it looked. One would think it shone of itself. Was there a soul in it too?

There was that bird again – if it was a bird. *Oh why wouldn't Billy wake up?*

There was a yawn, and Elizabeth gasped with relief. For she knew it was a pretended yawn, the sort that finds out if anyone else is awake. She sat up, and at the sudden movement Billy caught his breath. Elizabeth heard it, though he tried to stifle it. Then Billy was afraid too.

They sat up and looked at each other, wide-eyed and white. They did not speak. They did not need to speak. A cloud drifted over the moon, but the white iris shone none the less, ghostly even in the dark. It was like a Presence in the room. It was a Presence. And somewhere outside the lost soul called.

Something in them seemed to snap. With one bound they were out of bed, and Billy had the iris in his hand and was out on the verandah. Elizabeth followed, shivering. The moon came out again, riding very high and stately.

The moors were quiet; but they were not asleep. They lay and watched. Far out on the moors was a cleft like a darker shadow. Billy set down the iris and held out his hands to them.

'*Gomen nasai*,' he began, '*gomen nasai*... I did not know... You shall have them tomorrow, as soon as it is light... I did not know... We didn't know.'

Then fell a great silence. The bird had stopped calling. And the moon went back into its cloud.

With a great long breath Billy turned in. Elizabeth scurried after, and stood a little forlorn in the middle of the floor. Billy eyed her judicially over the hump of his knees.

'Want to come into my bed?' he asked without prejudice.

'I do,' said Elizabeth in a gasp. He made room, still judicially: but when she fell asleep it was with a handful of his pyjamas clutched firmly in one hand.

It was growing grey when she wakened, to find Billy already out of bed and half-dressed. In five minutes they had crawled down the creaking stairs, and were out of the house. The cold dew on the long grass brushed against their bare feet, and Billy plunged his face into the wisteria for the sake of its freshness. The sun had not yet risen. They had stepped into a strange world. They had not thought the moors could look so grey, but they had lost that uncanny watchfulness. There was an old hoary benevolence about them, and as they struck the road a grass-hopper shirred sleepily. He was just waking up.

'What's that?' said Billy suddenly. He stopped and pointed to where the bypath from the village struck the road. Shadowy figures came down it, moving slowly. They were carrying something and chanting, a broken monotone that fell away and took breath and went on again. They were nearer now, and Billy saw that they were dressed in white.

'It's a funeral,' he whispered, shakily. Elizabeth clutched at his hand and he drew back with that small desperate pressure to where the unseen brook by the roadside slipped through the long grass. They waited. The broken chant and the irregular footfalls came nearer: now and then the silent water whispered against a stone.

Slowly the little procession came abreast, and went halting past. It was an old priest who led the way, chanting the prayers for the dead, his shaven crown bowed over his beads: he walked a little fully, and now and then his voice quavered high and broke. Behind him came the coffin, the rude wooden shrine in which the poor bury their dead. When Prince Sanjo died, there were fifty men to carry him, and his white shrine rode high among white lotus flowers, like the passing of a god. But here there were only two. Jinricksha-men they were: that was why the funeral had to be so early. They had their day's work before them, these two, and they had shortened the night that was short enough already to carry their comrade on his last road. Then came the mourners: an old man dragging along with the listless step of one who has no need to make haste for anything any more: and close upon his heels a pair of children. They were no older than the twins: hand in hand they went, Bo-chan with his face set even as his grandfather's, for no Japanese will wear his heart on his sleeve: but now and then the little sister stumbled as she went and caught her breath in a small gasping sob. That was all.

It was the pitiful smallness of it that wrung Elizabeth's heart. She edged closer. Billy nodded fiercely. 'Come on.' he said, with a jerk of his head to the road. 'It'll make it look bigger.' Then after a long silence, 'It's O Riku san.'

Something about the old man's back was familiar. Elizabeth, plodding behind him, began to remember a certain *Kurumayasan*, very lean and gaunt and brown, who had carried their luggage from the railway station across the moor. He had stayed to supper with Sanagi-san, and eaten a great deal of rice and *shoyu*, and had cracked an immense number of jokes: and when their mother found that he had two children and gave him the persimmons the twins had meant to eat on the train but forgot because of the number and variety of the tunnels, the wrinkles of his brown face became a map of delight. He was the leanest and cheerfullest of all the *Kurumayasans* who sat in the broiling heat outside the little hill-station, and waited the coming of the mid-day train from Tokio. O Riku san lived with his father O Ji san, and his wife was dead. In the winter when no foreigners come to Karuizawa and the hotel is dead, he carved ivory, the marvellous ivory carving that is sold in Kuhn's great curio store in Yokohama and the Tokio Kankobas, branches of cherry blossom and demons, and warlike crabs. But the summer he spent between the shafts of his jinricksha, trotting stout foreigners up and down the Karuizawa roads, or hauling their trunks to and from the station with one or other of his brown *confrères*, heartening each other, or the one pulled and the other pushed, with that curious melancholy answering chant which to those who remember cadences, is one of the rarest incantations of the East. It was a hard life, but it paid better than the ivory carving. That was left to O Ji san to go on with, sitting all day beside the *hibachi* in the dim little house with the smoke-blackened oaken rafters, while the charcoal waned and glowed in its bed of white ash, and the children teased Neko san, the pussycat, with a white face like a foreigner and no tail. Until one day O Riku san strained his heart on the hill above the station. This was the end.

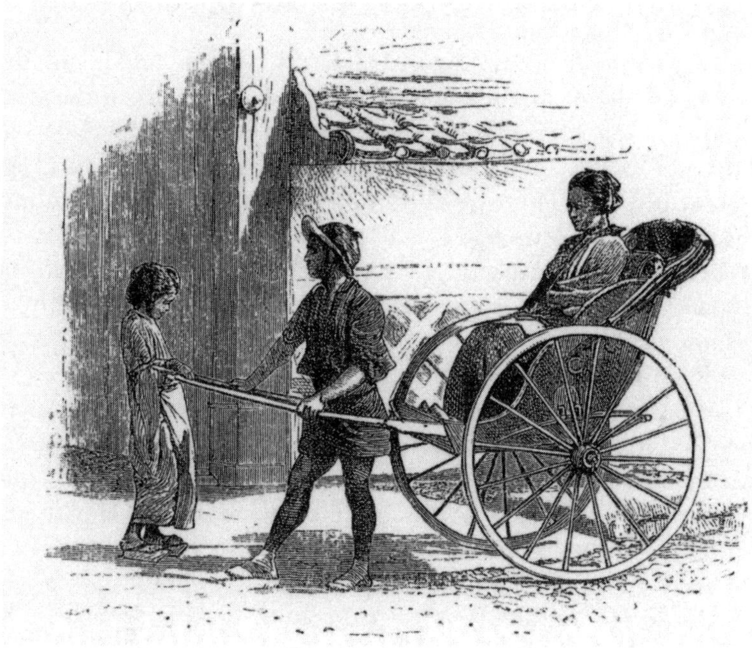

A *kuruma*.

Again there came the small choking sob. The old man looked round, and the depression lifted for a moment from his tired old face. So the foreigners had heard of it and come. After all, O Riku san was not to be forgotten in his death. His glance fell on the white iris, white for sorrow, and the light grew brighter in his eyes. O Riku san was indeed to be mourned as he should.

The daylight had broadened, but the moors were still grey when they reached the hollow. The kindly coolies had come after sundown and made all ready. It does not take very long to bury a *Kurumayasan*. '*Namu Amida Butsu*! *Namu Amida Butsu*!' droned the old priest, as they covered up the little shrine with the dry tangled sods. Elizabeth had devoutly shut her eyes. She saw the great bronze Buddha at Shiba with the quiet face and the heavy eyelids. Would he know that a *Kurumayasan* had strained his heart on the moors?

It was all over: all but the placing of the offerings that were to cheer the soul as it fared on its way to the *meido*, the shadowy land of the dead. The

Kurumayasans stepped back, as though giving place to the stranger. A little awkwardly, Billy knelt and laid the white iris on the sods. The *Kurumayasans* grunted inarticulate approval. Then O Ji san stumbled forward, fumbling in his sleeve for the little packet that he laid upon the grave. It was a roll of rice carefully wrapped up in seaweed, a great delicacy among the hills: but it looked very small and very poor in the still grey dawn: sorry comfort for one who [must] take a long journey.

And something of it must have struck O Ji san. He had begun the time-old prayer for the dead, the cry for their safe keeping that is the same in all ages; but even as he spoke his eye fell upon his poor provision, and the thought of O Riku san's disappointment smote upon his heart. He stood a moment irresolute, looking at it: then on a sudden he was on his knees, his shaking hands outstretched.

'O Riku san, O Riku san…it is so small… O my son, I had meant… And now thou will go hungry to the *meido*…thou wast so often hungry…'

Perhaps that was why O Riku san was so very lean. Perhaps that was why O Riku san was going to the *meido* so soon.

There broke from Billy one great rending sob. With a blind rush he was at the old man's side, and tumbling into his astonished hands whatever was in two trouser pockets. It was more than usual, for the twins had been saving for weeks to buy the little white owl down in Daiku san's, the carpenter's, and had got the sum, all but two *sen*, last night. But O Ji san was already on his feet.

'No, Little Honourable One, no', he said, bowing with his old world Japanese courtesy. 'O Riku san will understand…he will understand.'

'Take it', cried Billy, sobbing unashamed. 'It will buy him hot *mammé*, and *tofu* – and bean cakes. And he will soon, oh soon, [be] at the *meido*.'

O Ji san wavered. Then raising the money to his head in the old graceful fashion, he bowed low. 'The Little Honourable One is very good', he said gravely, and Billy fled.

He was quiet when Elizabeth overtook him, and they went home together. The moors were brighter, and a soft wind blew. After all, it was not so ill a day to fare to the *meido*. And suddenly the sun rose.

From somewhere near them a lark startled, and swept up singing. It was still singing when they reached home. On the upper verandah they saw their father pacing up and down, bareheaded in the early sunlight, the first astir. They knew by the sound that he was saying the Hebrew psalms – it was one of the familiar noises of the morning in that household – and they sat down on the steps to wait. There fell a silence and he began again: in English this time, but still with the Chinese scholar's trick of reading to himself to catch the tones. It was no more than a murmur at first: suddenly it rose to a chant —

'I am the Resurrection and the Life: he that believeth in me, though he were dead, yet shall he live.'

The lark was still singing, somewhere out of sight.

Notes

'Hanarisan [Hanare-*yama*]': Mount Hanare. The name does not refer to snakes, but means 'separate' or 'detached'. Basil Hall Chamberlain and W. B. Mason's contemporary guidebook states: 'On its E. side, near the summit, is a large cave inhabited by bats,' *Handbook for Travellers in Japan* (London: John Murray, 1891) p. 143. This may have been the source of the 'bad' association. However, Margaret records in her diary, on 24 June 1899, that 'Willie and George went up Hanare Yama yesterday.'

'the iris': The flowers are difficult to identify, and may have been described with poetic licence. *Kakitsubata*, or rabbit-ear iris (*Iris laevigata*), grows in boggy areas throughout Japan, and blooms from late spring to summer. Generally wild irises are purple.

'Engineering College': Presumably a red-brick building, like other Western structures.

'Campo Santo': The cemetery in Genoa where Constance Wilde was buried.

'Fujisan [Fuji-*san*]': Mount Fuji, as before.

'Sanagi san [Sanagi-*san*]': 'Sanagi', though somewhat unusual as a family name, suggests itself as the proper name of the Waddells' ubiquitous housekeeper 'Sneg'. From Margaret's diary we know that Sneg accompanied the family to Kamakura and Karuizawa, and also that she had a son.

'*daikon*': A giant radish, used to make the pickles that were eaten with rice.

'*andon*': A paper lantern, as described.

'*samurai*': When the clans were dispersed at the beginning of the Meiji period, the warrior class lost their traditional stipend, and had to find other means of support. The wearing of swords was also forbidden.

'Miss Van Bilt': In fact the manuscript has 'Miss Youngman', which has been adjusted here for the sake of consistency. A word has also been added to the next sentence to fill an apparent gap.

'Tale of the Forty-Seven Ronin': Japan's most celebrated story, many times retold and a staple of traditional theatre. It is a tale of revenge when, after their honourable master has been insulted at court, unduly provoked to anger, then ordered to die by his own hand, his forty-seven loyal followers bide their time until the opportunity comes for them to kill their master's enemy. When the deed has been accomplished, they all commit *harakiri*, as their master had done. *Rōnin* are masterless samurai, and the loyalty of these is taken as a paradigm.

'"*Gomen nasai*…"': 'We beg your pardon.'

'dressed in white': White is traditionally associated with death, though for a Buddhist funeral the bearers might have worn blue coats. The body was folded into a squatting position and buried in a tub-like coffin.

'Prince Sanjo': Prince Sanjō Sanetomi (1837–91), who belonged to a subsidiary branch of the Imperial Family. His funeral is described by Mary Crawford Fraser, *A Diplomat's Wife in Japan: Letters from Home to Home* (London: Hutchinson, 1900). pp. 535–45. Waddell could only have heard or read about this event.

'Jinricksha-men': Rickshaw-men. See the note on the first story.

'Bo-chan [*botchan*]': A boy, as before.

'O Riku san [*o*-Riku-*san*]': The name is problematic. The typescript favours 'Rike', while the handwritten version seems to be 'Riku', which has been taken. But in either case the name seems improbable, and the honorific *o* is inappropriate.

'*Kurumayasan* [*kuruma-ya-san*]': See the note for the previous story.

'*shoyu* [*shōyu*]': Soy sauce.

'O Ji san [*o-jī-san*]': Grandfather, an old man, as before.

'Kankobas [*kankōba*]': Bazaars. See the note earlier on Shiba.

'*hibachi*': Brazier or firebox.

'Neko san [*neko-san*]': The cat, as stated.

'*Namu Amida Butsu!…*': 'Save us, merciful Buddha!' or, in the case of a funeral, 'May he rest in peace.' (Lit. 'I take refuge in the Amida Buddha.')

'*meido*': Hades, the underworld, as indicated.

'Daiku san's [*daiku-san*]': The carpenter's, as stated.

'two *sen*': Two cents. See the note on the first story.

'*mammé* [*mame*]': Beans or peas.

PART 2:

The Spoiled Buddha:
Tales of Imagination

The Spoiled Buddha (prose version)

Binzuru is not sanctified; he is only popular. When Buddha and the fifteen Rakkan sit inside the chancel, Binzuru sits outside. The fifteen Rakkan are the disciples whom Gautama chose that he might impart to them the Doctrine, and now being made perfect in holiness and the extinction of desire, they are even as Buddha. They sit with him in the half-light behind the chancel grating, where the altar is blue with incense smoke and vibrant with prayer intoned, and the worshippers come and go with unshod feet. But Binzuru sits in the outer court where the wooden geta click all day on the pavement, and the light is broad, and strident with much conversation. Once there were sixteen Rakkan, but Binzuru was the sixteenth.

It is so long ago that he has almost forgotten it himself; yet once Binzuru was indeed a saint, and one whose feet were far advanced upon the Way. Then came the day that he sat, and a fellow-disciple with him, and contemplated the Infinite. The name of the fellow-disciple has not been preserved, but it may well have been Daruma, Daruma the Legless, who still sits near Binzuru, the chancel screen between. He is called the Legless because, having sat in contemplation of the Infinite for a matter of nine centuries, his lower limbs dropped off, being atrophied by disuse; or, as Daruma would have put it, if the fact had been brought to his notice, were themselves absorbed into the Infinite Negation. This, however, was centuries after the backsliding of Binzuru.

Binzuru sat and contemplated. Always when possible the disciples sat under a fig tree to contemplate. Gautama established the precedent; also it casts a broad and quiet shadow. This day the shadow was grey and dead in a world that was white with heat. Binzuru saw through half-closed eyes the universe sweep from him in rhythmic colourless waves. A woman came through the grove and stepped into the sunlight on the road. She swayed as she went. Binzuru saw her pass. The waves still rose and fell, but they were no longer colourless. Binzuru's eyes went after her. Gradually the world steadied itself; she was the only thing that swayed. Binzuru still gazed after her, not knowing what he did; then in his abstraction he spoke aloud. He said, 'She is very beautiful.'

Now Daruma the Legless had not perceived the woman; seeing, he saw not; but his moral perceptions are delicate. Daruma is very sensitive to the approach of evil. The voice of Binzuru came to him from a great way off, but it conveyed to him with an intimate shuddering that his sainted brother was overtaken of mortal sin. Daruma rose to his feet; the way lay very straight before him. He went and told the Buddha.

Then was the Buddha in perplexity. For he loved Binzuru; Binzuru indeed was always popular; but there was no blinking the facts. Had Binzuru been overtaken by his fault in a state of perfection less absolute, he might in time have retrieved himself; but to have attained to the perception of the Infinite, and to be side-tracked by the perception of a woman, is to sin against light, and argues a certain spiritual incapacity. Binzuru was disgraced. Yet, as I have said, Binzuru was a favourite with Gautama, and the Master cast about for some alleviation of the punishment. Thanks to his unfortunate dialectic, Binzuru had cast in his lot with the flesh; always must he cleave thereto. Might it not then be given him to cure all fleshly ills? Gautama knew that these are but part of the Great Illusion; knew also that the desire to escape from ill is itself the only ill; but also he knew that this knowledge is for the few, and that, for the many, toothache and a 'profound sciatica' are illusions singularly tenacious. He summoned Binzuru and explained to him the way; and Binzuru bowed himself and went out.

So, then, Binzuru sits outside the chancel, and all day the faithful throng him. He is very accessible. When Bochan has burnt his small fingers with hot beans at the temple stalls, he comes and rubs the fingers of Binzuru, and the smarting is eased. When a Kurumaya san has strained himself between the shafts of the jinricksha, he comes and rubs the thigh of Binzuru, and goes away halting no longer. Binzuru may never have been handsome, and centuries of believing friction have effaced all expression from his features save a benevolence perhaps a little vacuous. Little blinded children are brought to Binzuru, and the mother rubs the deep-set hollows through which Binzuru once looked upon the Infinite, and then lays her fingers upon the inflamed eyelids; but even as she does it she is exhorting the child to behold the countenance, not of ugly, kind Binzuru, but of the impassive Amida who sits beyond. It is a little hard.

For the cravings and agonies of the spirit, one does not come to Binzuru; his limitations are very definite. One goes within the chancel, to gaze upon the massive silver lotus, and at the knees of Buddha to be still. Nor do the young girls come to Binzuru; they too pass him, to go beyond the chancel grating and kneel at the feet of Kwannon the Compassionate, and pray for a lover from that Goddess of infinite comprehension. Binzuru's time will come

– when marriage has humbled them, and the akambo's small person is distended with the colic.

It is a question whether Binzuru regrets. Life is crowded in the outer court, and infinitely varied. It is dark behind the chancel screen, not to say stuffy. Binzuru wonders sometimes if they do not find it dull. Binzuru never finds it dull; he is too much interested. When a Kurumaya san has got a 'Jin Shimbun' from his fare, and reads it aloud to the other Kurumaya sans, Binzuru listens, and hears all about the political situation. Binzuru always listens; he knows all the gossip of Asakusa, and the rights of the squabbles among the priests, and the quarrelsomeness of the wife of Matsuda. Inside the chancel the Buddhas hear naught but prayer, and prayer intoned at that; it surely tends to grow monotonous. Binzuru hears everything – the tinkling of the bells outside the chancel, the awestruck remarks of the pilgrims from the country, the joking of the Kurumaya sans, the atheistical conversation of the young men from the Imperial University. This especially delights him. Binzuru's sense of humour is abnormally keen.

It is at night, if ever, that Binzuru has leisure for retrospect. It is certainly lonely at night, when the court is emptied of worshippers, and the stall-keepers have trundled away, and the priests are to bed. Inside the chancel the candles burn low and the incense sticks smoulder, and the Buddhas talk to one another, discoursing of high matters, of the Doctrine and the Law. But snatches only of their conversation reach to where Binzuru sits, alone and in the dark. In one sense it is his opportunity, and he might return with profit to his contemplation of the Infinite; but the broad forehead of contemplation has cured so many centuries of headache that now it recedes a little, and Binzuru has no longer the capacity for abstraction, if indeed he has the will. And this is doubtful. Sometimes he chuckles to himself over the exceedingly profane joke made by the seller of hot beans, to the seller of incense-sticks, and overheard by him that afternoon. He likes to picture himself shouting it over the screen to Daruma. And sometimes of a moonlight night, though of late it has happened seldom, he sees again the swaying of the shoulders that cost him the Bodhisat.

Notes

'Rakkan [*rakan*]': Arhats; the first disciples of Gautama, the Buddha; they are usually represented in the number of either sixteen or 500.

'unshod feet': Footwear is discarded before entering a temple.

'geta [*geta*]': Wooden clogs or sandals.

'Daruma': Bodhidharma (AD 470–543). See the Introduction, p. 28. It is unlikely that Daruma would be represented in a temple for the worship of Kannon.

'fig tree': The bo tree, which is sacred to Buddhists as the tree under which the Buddha

first attained enlightenment; also known as the pipal, it is a variety of tall fig (*Ficus religiosa*) native to India.
'Bochan [*botchan*]': A boy, as elsewhere.
'Kurumaya san [*kuruma-ya-san*]': A rickshaw-man, as before.
'jinricksha [*jin-riki-sha*]': Rickshaw, as before.
'Amida': Amitabha (lit. 'Immortal Light'); an enlightened form of the Buddha.
'akambo [*akambo*]': A baby.
'"Jin Shimbun" [*Jin Shimbun*]': The name of a newspaper (lit. 'People Paper').
'Bodhisat': The chance to become a bodhisattva, or enlightened spirit.

Buddhist priests

THE SPOILED BUDDHA

A PLAY IN TWO ACTS
BY HELEN WADDELL

DUBLIN	LONDON
The Talbot Press	T. Fisher Unwin
(LTD.)	(LTD.)
89 Talbot Street	1 Adelphi Terrace

1919

Title page of the published play.

The Spoiled Buddha: A Play in Two Acts

This play was produced at the Grand Opera House, Belfast, by the Ulster Theatre in February 1915

Prologue

(*Spoken by a Buddhist priest*)

The play is about the Buddha, in the days when he became a god: and about Binzuru, who was his favourite disciple, and who might have become even as the Buddha, only that he saw a woman passing by, and desired her beauty, and so fell from grace. The scene of the first Act is the Sacred Grove of Buddha, and the time is five hundred years before Christ was born. The scene of the second Act is the outer court of the Temple at Asakusa, which is a great temple in Japan, and the time is the present day. Though the interval between the first Act and the second is only so long as the actors shall be painting their faces, remember when the curtain rises again that two thousand four hundred years have gone by: that the Buddha is a great god worshipped in his temple, and the image of Binzuru has grown old outside the holy place.

For the rest, we leave it to our actors and your patience.

Characters

Act I

THE BUDDHA	
BINZURU	His favourite disciple
DARUMA	Binzuru's rival
FOURTEEN RAKKAN	The other disciples
THREE WOMEN FROM THE VILLAGE	
A BEAUTIFUL WOMAN	

Act II

THE BUDDHA	
BINZURU	
DARUMA	
RAKKAN	
PRIESTS	
THE SELLER OF INCENSE-STICKS	
THE SELLER OF HOT BEANS	
TWO KURUMAYASANS (JINRICKSHA-MEN)	
TWO YOUNG GIRLS	

Time Act I. THE SIXTH CENTURY BEFORE CHRIST
Act II. THE PRESENT

Act I

Time: The sixth century BC.
Scene: The Sacred Grove of Buddha. A broad pathway crosses the stage, disappearing among the trees. In the background, a clear space and a low broad stone. Sunlight on the road. There is a sound of far-off chanting and at intervals the boom of a Buddhist gong. The sound comes nearer. Enter the sixteen Rakkan in procession, chanting, the Buddha alone and last. They sit in a semi-circle, the Buddha on the stone of Enlightenment, cross-legged in the traditional attitude, the finger of exhortation raised. Binzuru and Daruma are on either hand. Silence.

Buddha. Hear, O Rakkan. To live is to desire.
Binzuru (*groaning*). O Master, it is true.
Daruma (*sharply*). What saidst thou?
Buddha. To live is to desire. Is it not so, O Daruma?
Daruma. I have not found it so.
Binzuru (*cheerfully*). This also is true. Daruma is a fish. Never in his life hath he desired anything, save the confounding of me. Is it not so, O Daruma?
Buddha. Peace, Binzuru. If Daruma were born a Buddha, jape not.
One of the Rakkan. Master, what is it to be born a Buddha?
Buddha. I know not. At a great cost obtained I this freedom.
One of the Rakkan. Master, how?
Buddha. Hear, O Rakkan. I dug out desire by the roots, as a man digs to uproot the bamboo. I cut the thongs of hunger and delight. So was my soul set free. So I achieved Nirvana.
Another of the Rakkan. Master, what is Nirvana?
Buddha. It is the Death of Death. It is the vision of the Infinite. It is peace.
Binzuru. Master, this Infinite – is it in great grey rings that sway…so (*he balances his hands*)…and the affairs of the world go by like duckweed in a river?
Buddha. Even so.
Binzuru (*triumphantly*). Then I have seen the Infinite.
Buddha. When, Binzuru?
Binzuru. Years ago. Before I set my feet upon the Way of the Buddhas. O Master, it is a stony way.
Buddha (*indulgently*). And what was thy way?
Binzuru. See you, O Master, it is like this. One must first be well drunken. (*Daruma half rises, but the Buddha motions him down.*) One fixes one's eye upon an object. A small object, a round object. And contemplates.

And the world falls into rings…that sway. Twice have I done it. Once it was the brim of my *saké* cup…and once the rim of my pipe bowl. But (*ruefully*) when I entered on the Way, I renounced these things. And, Master, the Infinite has gone with them.

Daruma (*angrily*). Master, wilt thou suffer him?

Buddha. Peace, Daruma. Binzuru, I fear thy jest is dearer to thee than was thy *saké*. Nevertheless thou hast done well to renounce the last. For hear, O Rakkan. There be three desires, the desire of life, the desire of wine –

(*The Rakkan on the outer edge of the semi-circle has a view of the pathway from the village. He holds up a warning hand. Women's voices and laughter and the tinkle of a samisen.*)

Rakkan. Master, there be women from the village approaching.

Buddha. Thou didst well to stay me. It is not good that the words of the Law should be spoken in the hearing of women.

(*He lapses into the immemorial attitude, the eyes heavy-lidded and down-cast. All the Rakkan copy him, save Binzuru, who twirls his thumbs and looks down the road, and Daruma, who furtively watches Binzuru. Three women pass, laughing and talking among themselves. They tinkle the samisen as they go by. They eye the Buddhas, and the girl with the samisen looks back over her shoulder, and strikes three of the laughing notes as they disappear. The Rakkan stir again, and Binzuru sighs.*)

Binzuru. Master, why is the Law forbidden them? Have they not souls to be saved?

Buddha. Yea, Binzuru. But it hath happened that in the saving of their souls a man hath lost his own. Hear, O Rakkan. There be three desires, and of them she is the deadliest. The Disturber of Integrity is she, the Entangler of the Upright, the Snare of the World. Let not the Buddhas look upon a woman –

Daruma (*leaning forward, that he may see the Buddha's face*). Master, what then of Kwannon?

(*The Buddha starts slightly, then recovering himself gazes before him, darkened and lowering. Binzuru scowls at Daruma.*)

Daruma (*smoothly*). Not for myself, Most August, would I ask it. But there are evil-minded persons – In my hearing it hath been said that in the matter of Kwannon the Buddha did not practise as he preaches. And I would have wherewith to stop the mouth of the adversary.

Binzuru (*truculently*). Stop it with –

Buddha (*raising his head and speaking haltingly*). Peace, Binzuru. It may be that Daruma hath wisely spoken. It is an old tale and an evil. Of that which was Kwannon's life it is not mine to speak. It has naught to do with me – or you. But this I know, that when for the sins of the flesh and her spirit she was cast into Hell, darkness became light about her – her beauty was very great – and Hell paradise. And the devils were wroth, and they took her, and bound her hand and foot, and flung her into the great slough that is between Hell and earth, deep mire where there is no standing; and the filth received her, and Hell was Hell again, and the light darkness. But after many months, on the side of it nearest the earth…I saw a lotus growing in the mire…and one morning, as I passed that way, I saw the cup was opened. And in it…her body… (*His voice dies into silence. The Rakkan sit forward straining. Binzuru has forgotten even Daruma.*)

Binzuru (*breathlessly*). And?

Buddha (*rousing himself*). I found her…and made plain to her the Way…the Way of the Buddhas. And already has she reached Nirvana. Wherefore, Binzuru (*he turns, indulgent and whimsical*), have patience, and thou too shalt some day…if the spirit be willing. (*He rises, followed by the Rakkan.*)

Binzuru (*ruefully*). The spirit, Master, yea! But the flesh!

(*The Rakkan form in procession, and the chant is about to begin when Daruma turns to the Buddha.*)

Daruma. Master, I would stay that I may meditate alone.

(*The Buddha nods in silence. Exit the Rakkan in procession. Daruma settles himself under a tree by the roadside, and sits motionless, gazing before him. The chanting dies away. There is a great stillness. Enter Binzuru. He saunters up the road in the glare of the sun. He stops before Daruma, surveying him. Daruma is in shadow.*)

Binzuru (*approvingly*). Nice little spot. Cool. Very.

(*Daruma withers him, without moving.*)

Binzuru. Contemplating? The Infinite? (*He mops his forehead.*)

Daruma (*hollowly*). Trouble me not.

Binzuru (*earnestly*). Not for the world. (*He sits down beside him, and waits until Daruma is again composed.*) Got it again Daruma?

Daruma. What?

Binzuru. The Infinite.

(*Daruma ignores him.*)

Binzuru (*pleasantly*). Because I would give you counsel, Daruma. Good counsel. Next time you get your eye on the Infinite, keep it there, and (*with sudden belligerence*) leave the Buddha alone.

Daruma (*stirring uneasily*). There are evil-minded persons –

Binzuru (*genially*). There are. Minds like a carrion-crow. Like yours, Daruma. (*He settles himself more comfortably.*) Never take exercise, Daruma?

Daruma. For months together I have not flickered an eyelid nor uncrossed my legs.

Binzuru. Bad for you, Daruma. Bad for you. That explains it, O man of bile. Bad for your legs too. They'll wither up. Wither up and drop off. (*He stretches his own legs before him and surveys them tenderly. They are good legs.*)

Daruma. It matters little how soon my legs, or I with them, are absorbed into the Infinite Negation.

Binzuru (*eyeing the legs of Daruma critically*). You may be right, Daruma. You may be right.

(*He crosses his own in the canonical attitude, folds his hands on his stomach and looks straight before him. The drollery vanishes from the eyes and the lines of the mouth. Slowly his face becomes rapt. Silence.*

(*Women's voices and laughter and the tinkle of a samisen, very far off. Binzuru does not hear. He is so placed that his eyes are on the unseen stretches of the road, but there is no consciousness in them. Silence.*

(*Binzuru's face changes. Some one is approaching not yet seen by the audience. It is the same absorption with which he looked on the Infinite, but more rapturous. A woman comes in sight. She is beautiful, and sways as she comes. She is carrying a jar on her head, and one arm is raised to steady it. Binzuru leans forward, devouring her, but she does not lift her eyes. All this while Daruma has sat motionless, unseeing. She passes, and Binzuru turns sideways, still following her with his eyes. He has risen on his knees, his arms outstretched.*)

Binzuru (*brokenly*). Thy beauty – (*He sinks back.*)

(*Daruma sits up with a jerk. His face livens with scandalised malevolence. He turns and looks at the unconscious Binzuru, bends forward, and looks quickly down the road. Then he nods his head twice, gathers his garments from touching his brother, and is about to hurry off when the boom of the returning gong strikes on his ear. He nods with satisfaction, and stands listening. Binzuru winces at the sound like a man struck in his sleep; he rises and goes slowly across the stage, his eyes wide open and fixed, like one unwilling to break a dream. Daruma watches him till he disappears. The sound of the gong comes very near. Enter the Rakkan in procession, the Buddha at their head. Daruma springs forward.*)

Daruma. Master! Master! That such things should be! Our sainted brother – overtaken – of mortal sin!

(*He is gesticulating. Intense and pleased interest on the faces of the Rakkan. The Buddha motions him aside, paces forward to the daïs, and sits down deliberately. The Rakkan follow him.*)

Buddha. Now, Daruma, thou mayst unburden thyself.

Daruma. Master, we sat thus by the road, he and I; I perceiving the Infinite, he twirling his thumbs. And behold, a woman passed down the road, swaying as she went –

Buddha. How comes it that thou didst see her, if thine eyes were on the Infinite?

Daruma. Master, I did not see her, then. My soul was as a kite, tossing among grey clouds. But the voice of my brother in speech with her grappled me, and the lewdness thereof was as a rough hand on the string that jerked me back to the world.

Buddha. Of what then dost thou accuse thy brother?

Daruma (*drawing himself up*). He, a Buddha, has looked upon a woman and found her fair. He is sinner of mortal sin. (*He raises his arm. Stridently*) Let him be cast out!

All the Rakkan (*rising, and with the same gesture*). Let him be cast out!

(*The Buddha gazes sombrely before him. There is a rustle and nudging among the Rakkan. They crane forward. Binzuru is coming down the road, rapt, unseeing, swaying as he comes, his hands balancing up and down before him, smiling a little foolishly. He appears to see no one, is still walking in a dream. The Buddha watches him, then turns upon the Rakkan.*)

Buddha. Go.

(*They rise mutinously, looking at one another and at the Buddha. He sits unmoved. They form sullenly and march out, Daruma alone and last. Meanwhile Binzuru continues his progress. The Buddha watches him sadly.*)

Buddha. Binzuru.

(*Binzuru comes to himself, somewhat dazed. He turns to the Buddha, rapturous.*)

Binzuru. Master, I have perceived the Infinite.
Buddha. Thou hast perceived a woman.

(*Binzuru stops short. Slow realisation dawns upon his face. He is puzzled and piteous.*)

Binzuru. Master, what have I done?
Buddha. Thou hast looked upon a woman to lust after her. It is Daruma who says it. Is this thing true?
Binzuru (*stands thinking*). Master…I know not. It was this way. We sat together, in the shadow, he and I. But I forgot him. Master, I saw the Infinite. It was grey…but with the greyness of a pearl. Then she came…afar off…and I saw her not, but the greyness was suffused…it glowed… like a pearl when it lies on a woman's flesh. (*The Buddha raises a warning hand. Binzuru nods hastily.*) She came nearer, and the grey waves slipped back. And nearer… And at last there was nothing but herself in all the world. She passed by, and I looked before me, and saw nothing, and heard nothing, and of what befell thereafter I can tell nothing. Of myself I had no knowledge, until…until your voice brought back my soul.

(*There is silence for a long while.*)

Buddha (*slowly*). Thou hast seen the Infinite. It is true, Binzuru, and I would it were not. For to have seen the Infinite, and to be distracted from it by the Finite, by a woman, is to sin against light.
Binzuru. But, Master, she glorified the Infinite.
Buddha. For how long?

(*Silence.*)

Binzuru (*unwillingly*). Until she drew near.

(*He stands, his head sunk on his breast. The Buddha gazes before him. At last he turns and looks down the road by which the Rakkan departed.*)

Buddha. They, thy brethren, demand that thou be cast out.
Binzuru (*falling on his knees*). Master, not that! I will go down many degrees in the Scale of Virtue. I will humble myself – even to the feet of Daruma. Let me not be cast out!
Buddha. Thou didst see, and didst look away. Thyself shall judge whether thou art of the Buddhas or no. It is not I who give or take away.
Binzuru (*desperately*). Did not Kwannon the harlot –
Buddha. Kwannon!

(*It is almost a cry. Binzuru checks himself at the sound of it. He gazes at the Buddha, wonderingly. At last the Buddha recovers himself, but he does not look at Binzuru.*)

Buddha. If...Kwannon...sinned, it was before her feet were set upon the way.

(*Binzuru watches him, with dawning comprehension. He gets slowly to his feet.*)

Binzuru (*heavily*). It is enough. I will go.

(*He walks to the path, the Buddha watching him drearily. Just as he is turning down the road, the Buddha's face lightens.*)

Buddha. Binzuru! (*Binzuru turns, but makes no attempt to come back.*) It cannot be but thou shouldst go. And yet...I would not have thee far from me. Binzuru, thou hast cast in thy lot with the flesh. Always must thou cleave thereto. What and if I give thee power to cure all fleshly ills?

Binzuru. Master, there is no ill.

Buddha. Thou hast rightly said. Thou and I, we know that it is but part of the Great Illusion. But the multitude, Binzuru, that do not know... (*Whimsically*) Toothache – it is a tenacious illusion.

Binzuru (*bewildered*). O Master, it is true. But how shall I cure toothache?

Buddha (*gaily*). See you, Binzuru, thou shalt have efficacy in that same stubborn flesh of thine. The small ones shall come, that have burned their fingers in the fire, and rub thy fingers – so – and the smarting shall be eased. Likewise a profound sciatica –

Binzuru (*dismayed*). But, Master, they will rub me away!

Buddha (*more gravely*). Even so. So shalt thou work out thy salvation. Thou knowest, Binzuru, that they, the multitude, go about even now to build us a temple. I and the Rakkan shall sit inside the chancel. Thou, Binzuru, must sit without. But all day shall the faithful throng thee. And behold, the touch of faith will do from without what thyself couldst not from within. They will rub thee away, Binzuru, rid thee of thy unruly flesh. And so, in the end of the ages, thou too shalt achieve Nirvana. Till then – (*He raises his hand in benediction and farewell. Binzuru bows himself, and goes slowly out.*)

(*The Buddha watches him, long after he has disappeared. Then rousing himself, he moves over to the gong which the Rakkan have left standing, strikes a single note, and returns to the old attitude. The Rakkan return, looking this way and that, and whispering among themselves. They sit down, all but Daruma, who stands uncertainly, eyeing the coveted seat at the Buddha's right hand. He walks a pace towards it, stops, and eyes the Buddha.*)

Daruma (*pointing*). Master…the seat on thy right hand…is it empty?
Buddha. Thou seest it.
Daruma (*hesitating and moving uneasily*). Master…is it thy will that it remain empty?
Buddha. Thou hast said.

(*Daruma, scowling and chagrined, takes his old seat. The Rakkan stiffen into the Buddha's rigid pose.*)

CURTAIN

Act II

Time: The present day.

Scene: The outer court of the Temple at Asakusa. It is dusk in the court, but inside the chancel screen one sees the gleam of candle-light on the faces of the Buddha and the Rakkan, and the gold and red of lacquer work. The bronze figure of Binzuru is in the court, to the right of the chancel. He is cross-legged, his hands folded on his stomach. A few incense-sticks are smouldering before the chancel steps, and from inside comes the intermittent chant of the priests. Beside the low pedestal on which Binzuru sits a Kurumayasan is squatting, and reading the 'Jin Shimbun'. He is in dark blue, with the 'mon' of his craft in great white characters on his back. Opposite him to the left of the court sits the Seller of Incense-Sticks smoking, and beside him the Seller of Hot Beans, who is blowing the charcoal in his brazier. There are small bowls ranged before him.

Seller of Incense. The times are not good times.

Seller of Hot Beans. They are bad times.

Seller of Incense. What hast thou to grumble at, thou Seller of Hot Beans? This people are swine. They will buy hot beans to fill themselves, but they will not buy incense to fill the gods. Hardly a stick of incense have I sold this day.

Seller of Beans. It is the hand of the gods on thee for thy bad tongue. I told thee that the Buddhas would chastise it.

Seller of Incense. The Buddhas are asleep. They sleep loud. Hearken, and thou wilt hear them –

Seller of Beans. Hold thy peace. Half afraid am I to sit beside thee, lest the gods mistake me for thee.

Seller of Incense. They will not do that, O Man of Beans. Do not flatter thyself. See, O Kurumayasan (*he calls to the man behind the paper as another Kurumayasan limps into the court*), here is thy brother, nigh as light of foot as thou.

(*The lame Kurumayasan smiles broadly.*)

Kurumayasan. Greeting, O my brother. Greeting, O Man of Incense. Greeting, O Man of Beans.

Seller of Incense. What aileth thee, O Runner? Wouldst thou be taken for the Sacred Tortoise?

Kurumayasan. Thy tongue is as sharp as the edge of the bamboo grass. Yesterday I strained myself pulling a fat pig of a foreigner up the

Tori-i-zaka. And to-day I was two hours crawling hither. A–ah! (*He sits down with a grunt before Binzuru, and applies himself vigorously to rubbing the thigh of Binzuru alternately with his own.*)

Seller of Beans. There was a young man from the University. He said there was no virtue in Binzuru. That it was a lie of the priests. That a man might as well rub himself upon his own mats. What sayest thou, O Runner?

Kurumayasan. I say that the young man was a fool. It was but last week that the *akambo* had the colic, was swollen even as a paper lantern, and his mother brought him – Aha!

(*Two young girls pass into the court. The Seller of the Incense-Sticks and the Seller of Hot Beans and the two Kurumayasans eye them with satisfaction. They stop before the Seller of Incense shyly.*)

One of the Young Girls. How much?

Seller of Incense (*bowing*). Five *sen.*

(*They buy half-a-dozen. The Seller of Incense touches the pavement with his head, and they pass on. The Kurumayasan behind the paper grunts with appreciation.*)

Seller of Beans. Will that be for the Buddha now?

Seller of Incense (*derisively*). Nay, nor Binzuru either. They go to Kwannon – to pray for their lovers. The Buddha maketh no account of women. What, O Runner (*the lame Kurumayasan is on his feet and stepping gingerly*) art on thy legs again? May the devil possess me if thou art not as nimble as – Daruma! Peace, and I will tell thee a joke about Daruma. I thought on it last night in my bed.

(*The Seller of Hot Beans inclines to listen, and with him the appeased Kurumayasan. The Seller of Incense-Sticks speaks rapidly, with snorts of laughter. They fall apart into the diverse attitudes of a savoured jest. On their laughter breaks the deep booming of the temple gong, a single stroke, dominant and mournful. A priest, robed in yellow and with shaven crown, appears in the opening of the chancel screens. He makes the gesture of dismissal. The Sellers collect their wares, the Kurumayasan rises, leaving his paper on the ground, the young girls come hurrying from the farther shrine. In a little while the court is empty. The priests march chanting in procession from the chancel, round the court to the outer gates. There is a clash, as of their closing. The sound of chanting grows fainter. Silence. The incense-sticks before the chancel burn with a faint blue smoke; the twilight has deepened, but there is a glimmer of moonlight on the motionless figure of Binzuru. The rigidity of the bronze figure relaxes. He stretches his arms above his head with a luxurious yawn, and settles down to twirl his thumbs, contemplating them the while he smiles to himself. In a little while he chuckles, a reminiscent chuckle. He is so intent upon his thumbs that he does not see a figure advancing from inside the chancel. It is the Buddha himself, cumbrous and magnificent and stately, the golden boss of wisdom between his brows. He pauses for a moment in the opening of the chancel screens, moves slowly forward, and stands before Binzuru, watching him.*)

Buddha. Binzuru!

Binzuru (*starting violently*). Master! (*He struggles to get up.*)

Buddha. It is enough, Binzuru; we are no longer young.

Binzuru. It is not that. It is my back. Sciatica. They have me nearly hollow. But, Master (*he looks round, anxious to do the honours of the outer court*), where is there a – would you not sit down?

Buddha. In truth, Binzuru, I am tired sitting. (*He glances at the dim chancel.*)

Binzuru (*confidentially*). I wouldn't wonder. Exercise – nothing like it. Told Daruma so. Years ago. Centuries ago.

Buddha. But not to profit, Binzuru. He lost his legs. Nine hundred years ago.

Binzuru. Told him so. Told him so. Atrophy, they call it. Not that they were much loss. Said so myself. (*Binzuru surveys his own legs.*) And my own – marvellous the Kurumayasans and the wrestlers that come. Come here and rub me. Rub me away.

Buddha (*surveying him*). I had hardly thought it would be so soon. The stubborn flesh… Only another thousand years, Binzuru, and you shall sit with us again – yonder. (*He looks again at the chancel.*)

Binzuru (*terrified*). You – you think so?

Buddha (*laughing softly*). You are in no hurry, Binzuru?

Binzuru (*squirms; his voice lowers*). Master – your pardon – but – (*in a rush*) dost never find it…DULL?

(*The Buddha eyes the chancel.*)

Buddha. Speaking as one Buddha to another – (*Binzuru bridles and inclines his head.*) Speaking as one Buddha to another, Binzuru, it is dull. (*He eyes Binzuru very kindly.*) How long is it since you and I talked together, Binzuru?

Binzuru (*reflectively*). With the Great Cold it will be two thousand – two thousand four hundred years.

Buddha. I would have come before this, Binzuru. Many times. But Daruma – he never sleeps.

Binzuru. A marvellous man, Daruma. Marvellous man. But, Master, tonight?

Buddha. I discoursed, Binzuru –

Binzuru. I hear you sometimes. Snatches. Only snatches. Am getting deaf. Earache. So many cases.

Buddha. It was on the first chapter of the eighth book of the Vedas – you remember it, Binzuru?

Binzuru (*feelingly*). I do.

Buddha. And at last even Daruma slept. (*He looks round the court with pleased interest, and stoops to pick up the 'Jin Shimbun'.*) What is this, Binzuru? Is it a Sacred Writing?

Binzuru (*convulsed*). It is not. The Kurumayasans – they read it aloud to one another. I listen. I am always listening. I hear it all. The divorce cases. And the news from the Front. And politics – the political situation. (*He says it proudly.*)

Buddha. Politics? What are politics, Binzuru? Are they religious? Religious ceremonies?

Binzuru (*again convulsed*). They are not. Politics – Politics – (*he flounders*). They pass the time. They pass the time. Master (*eagerly*), take it, in your girdle, and read it. Tell Daruma it is Sacred Writing.

Buddha (*wistfully, looking from it to the chancel*). The light is bad, Binzuru. They burn so much incense. And my eyes –

Binzuru. Same with my own. And headache – (*he draws his hand across his forehead and shakes his head mournfully*). Master, they have all the good looks rubbed off me.

Buddha. See what it is to be popular, Binzuru.

Binzuru (*still grumbling, but affectionately*). There was a small one this morning burnt his tongue with the hot beans, yonder. He came and stood on me and licked me. And then he gave me his bib. This is it. He put it on me himself. (*He tugs at a pink wisp under his left ear. The Buddha stoops to inspect it. Then he straightens himself and looks down at Binzuru with immense affection.*)

Buddha (*teasingly*). And the young girls, Binzuru?

Binzuru (*mournfully*). Not for me. Not for me. I see them. But they go past old Binzuru.

Buddha (*indulgently*). Where, Binzuru? They do not come to us.

Binzuru. Yonder (*he jerks his head to the darkness behind him*), to Kwannon – (*he checks himself in confusion. The Buddha inclines his head gravely, as one who acknowledges information. He is apparently unaware of Binzuru's embarrassment. He gazes again about the court, then turns upon him with a gleam, as suddenly remembering.*)

Buddha. Tell me, Binzuru, what was it was in your mind as I came through the chancel?

Binzuru. (*lighting up*). It was a joke. The Seller of Incense-Sticks told it to the Seller of Hot Beans. It was a good joke. I was for shouting it over the

screen to Daruma just as you came out.
Buddha. That was fortunate. It would have wakened him.
Binzuru. It would, in soul. (*He rocks himself.*)
Buddha (*eyeing him wistfully*). Is it a good joke?
Binzuru (*struggling for gravity*). Master, it is a profane joke.
Buddha. Tell me, Binzuru.

(*Their heads come close. Binzuru whispers amid splutters of laughter behind his hand. Back goes the Buddha's head in a shout of laughter, stifled halfway by the sudden terror on Binzuru's face. They listen. Inside the chancel someone yawns, a comprehensive, waking yawn.*)

Binzuru (*hopelessly*). It is Daruma.

(*For a moment the Buddha stands stupefied. Then with a swing of his great shoulders he turns his back on the chancel and stands looking before him into the night. While one might count ten he stands to make decision. Then with a long breath he turns round and paces steadily toward the chancel, the while he begins in the voice of intoning.*)

Buddha. Now it is written in the first chapter of the eighth book of the Vedas that whoso hath attained to the perception of the Infinite can in no wise be ensnared –

(*There is a snore, gentle, long-drawn, continuous. Binzuru, who has been wagging his head in admiration, is silently convulsed. The Buddha pauses on the first step of the chancel, and turns to look at Binzuru. For a moment he shares the jest. Then gravity falls on him. He stands gazing at Binzuru. After a long pause he speaks, half to himself.*)

Buddha. Two thousand – two thousand four hundred years. Binzuru, the years are long years
Binzuru (*gravely*). They are long years.

(*Again there is silence. The Buddha turns his eyes from Binzuru, and looks into the night.*)

Buddha (*haltingly*). Binzuru – was she very beautiful?

(*Binzuru eyes him.*)

Binzuru. Beautiful? As Kwannon.

(*The Buddha turns and looks at Binzuru. For a while the two gaze at each other. It is the final comprehension. The Buddha turns to climb the steps, and paces into the chancel. Binzuru watches him till he disappears, then relapses into the old attitude.*)

CURTAIN

Notes

'Buddha': Gautama Siddhartha (c.563–c.483 BC), an Indian prince, whose teachings formed the basis of Buddhism.
'Binzuru': See the Introduction, passim.
'Daruma': See the note on the previous story.
'Rakkan [*rakan*]': See the note on the previous story.
'Kurumayasan [*kuruma-ya-san*]': Rickshaw-man, as before.
'Jinricksha-men': Rickshaw-men, as elsewhere.
'O Daruma': From here on, the 'O' seems to be more clearly used as an apostrophe.
'Nirvana': Bliss or transcendence resulting from the extinction of desire.
'samisen': A three-stringed Japanese musical instrument similar to a banjo; also known sometimes as a 'shamisen'.
'jar on her head': A gesture towards the Indian setting, despite the samisen above.
'"mon" [*mon*]': A family crest, such as that put on a kimono used for formal wear. It does not indicate a craft or guild, nor is it very large.
'Seller of Incense-Sticks…': All accounts, including that of Isabella Bird, stress the lively atmosphere and the variety of activities in the temple courtyard. See the Introduction, pp. 26–7.
'Sacred Tortoise': Perhaps Waddell was thinking of the turtle which, together with the crane often represented as standing on its back, is a symbol of longevity.
'Tori-i-zaka': A well-known slope not far from where the Waddells lived. It can be found in what is now Roppongi, and the name is unchanged. Tōyō Eiwa, the girls's school that Waddell attended, was located there and still exists.
'*akambo*': A baby, as before.
'five *sen*': Five cents. See earlier notes.
'touches the pavement with his head': Presumably he is kneeling on the ground beside his wares.
'robed in yellow': Saffron robes are common in other parts of Asia, but in Japan the robes of Buddhist priests are usually black or white.
'bib': 'Binzuru is a highly popular object of worship with the lower classes, and his image is often adorned by some of his devotees with a red or yellow cotton hood, a bib, and mittens,' wrote Basil Hall Chamberlain and W.B. Mason, *Handbook for Travellers in Japan* (London: John Murray, 1891), p. 28. Such practices are still observed today with statues of Jizō, the guardian of children.
'eighth book of the Vedas': This appears to be a fanciful quotation. The *Vedas* are an elaborate set of hymns in which the Infinite is seldom mentioned.

The Flowing Invocation

Shinzo sat cross-legged in the courtyard of his house and looked before him. The stream from the mountains slipped past him in the darkness, chuckling to itself: from the ricefields rose the croaking of the unwearied frogs. The paper shutters of his house were drawn; they glowed with the opaque radiance of a Chinese lantern. Figures went to and fro within, casting shadows. It reminded Shinzo of a toy that he had seen once in Tokio – a painted paper house that revolved round a candle. Inside the screens they were preparing the body of O Tsuyu san, his wife, for burial.

O Tsuyu san's name signified the dew of the morning. They had been married for a year, and she was dead in childbirth. It augurs ill for a woman when she dies in childbirth. Shinzo was not imaginative, but on that visit to Tokio he had seen the lacquer panels in the outer court of the temple at Asakusa, reproductions of the seven Buddhist hells. The seventh is the Lake of Blood, in which O Tsuyu san was even now drowning. Shinzo remembered the lacquer, red and black, and with it, inconsequently, the pitiful roundness of her chin.

A mosquito sang through the darkness, shrilling suddenly in his ear. He struck at it, and the small voice stopped. Shinzo was sorry. Remorse took him: he fell to wondering whose soul it was he had sent out again, in which hell it would expiate the short poisonous life. Or if the gods would let it be reborn again before they struck. One thing was certain: they would not forget. It might have been many rebirths since O Tsuyu san was a woman of evil life; but the gods had not forgotten, and to-day they had struck, and her soul would go down into the Lake of Blood until it was clean of that stain. Then it would begin again, after aeons of torment: some little life low down on the Wheel, without warning and without memory. The croaking in the ricefields rose to an ecstasy and the shadows on the screens were monstrous.

Presently their wavering ceased. There came a small sound of tapping: it was O Ba san his mother, emptying her pipe against the metal of the 'tabako-bon'. The screens slid apart and the neighbour women came out, groping in the dark below the verandah for their wooden clogs and lanterns, while O Ba san, squatted on her heels in the gap of the shutters, bowed her head to the floor and pursued the retreating guests with ceremonious leave-takings. There was a chorus of the 'Sayonara' ('Since it must be!') that makes even farewell in the East a compliment, and the women clicked past him on their high clogs, each with her swaying lantern, until the night received them. They did not see where he sat. The mother of Shinzo, peering into the darkness, detected in the shadow the motionless figure of her son. Her cracked treble rose querulously.

'Didst hear it, O Shinzo? The wife of the Maker of Tubs? But yesterday, and delivered of twins. And I had the offer of her for thee.'

The stolid figure made no sign of having heard. O Ba san shrilled higher.

'Hast thou no shame in thee, O Shinzo, to have brought such shame upon the house as never was in Sakai? To-morrow will the Flowing Invocation be set upon the brook yonder, that every evil-smelling seller of *daikon* that passes on the road may put up a prayer for her, and think pity on the man that took her to wife and the house where she brought to birth.'

Shinzo raised his heavy eyes. 'The Flowing Invocation?'

'Did I not say it?' cried O Ba san triumphantly. 'Never in thy memory hath there been need of it in Sakai. But once – hast thou no mind of it? – thou wert as high as a *tatami* is broad – I took thee to the hills, to the house of thy father's uncle at Mitamura. And we passed it on the road, and I made thee fill the dipper and pour water for the poor soul in torment. I had to hold thee up. Thou couldst not reach so high.'

The Flowing Invocation.

Slowly Shinzo remembered; a little mountain stream and a cloth flung across it, hung by the corners to four bamboo poles, a cloth with characters upon it and a weather-beaten tablet with the name of a woman dead. He remembered that he had filled the dipper that hung by it, and emptied it into the cloth, and said after his mother the great invocation, '*Namu yo, namu yo, ho ren ge Kyo*.' He remembered, too, how slowly the water had dripped through.

'Ay', said Shinzo. 'I remember. But what has that to do with – her?'

O Ba san eyed him half pityingly.

'The sooner thou hast set one up yonder, the better for her. See you, Shinzo, it is this way. Kwannon the Compassionate had a tenderness for women in her case – there be some that say that Kwannon herself…'

'It is not good', said Shinzo, 'to speak ill of the gods'.

O Ba san spread her hands. 'Under the candlestick', she said profoundly, 'is the darkest place. How so be it, Kwannon got leave of the Buddha that the like of O Tsuyu san should have pain in the Lake of Blood only so long as the Web of Expiation is wearing through. And every time the water is poured and the name of Buddha named, the web grows thinner. And when it wears a hole and the water drips readily, even so the soul slips through the net of hell.'

'And how long', asked Shinzo eagerly, 'might that be?'

O Ba san meditated.

'The one on the hills at Mitamura – it was nine years. But', hastily, 'it was a lonely spot and few passers-by. And one by the Great House of Owari. But she was a *daimyo*'s wife. It was six weeks.'

'How?'

O Ba san laughed a little contemptuously. 'Thou hast not much wit, Shinzo. Kwannon wove a web before she changed her world. It is kept in the temple at Nikko: so fine that the mists might drip through it. And the priests sell it. But not to the like of you.'

'What might the price of it be?'

Again O Ba san laughed.

'The *daimyo* at Owari paid a thousand yen. Thou hadst better go down to the temple and see what the priests will give thee for thyself, and thy father's house and all thou hast.'

Shinzo's head had sunk upon his breast. O Ba san eyed him, and turned in, drawing the screens behind her. She was sorry for Shinzo, but it was not her fault that she had borne a fool. How great a fool she had not realised. For that same night Shinzo did indeed go to the temple and drive his bargain with the priests. His house and his seven ricefields he mortgaged: sell it he could not, for his duty to his mother, which is piety, came before his duty to his wife, which is inclination. Also he bound himself three days in every month to serve as jinricksha-man in the temple festivals. For this they gave him a web which cost one hundred yen; not of Kwannon's weaving, but guaranteed of an admirable delicacy. Shinzo felt it all the way home between his fingers and thumb. His heart sank at the coarseness of it.

For a while they told stories further down the valley of a crazed man who stood knee deep in the Kanagawa and baled continuously, seeming to rest neither day nor night. At first he stooped between every dipperful and eyed the cloth anxiously where it sagged at the great name of Buddha. But experience taught him better. It only wasted time. Then on the evening of the thirteenth day O Ba san came out and, sitting on the bank, reproached him with the bitter reproaching of old age in the East. The baling slackened after that, and Shinzo went doggedly to the thinning of the rice in his fields, watching the road eagerly for passers-by. There were not many.

It lasted for eighty-seven days. Then came a night that Shinzo rose and came out an hour before dawn, as he was wont to do, and the brightening east found him squatted before the Flowing Invocation, the dipper idle beside him. A devil had possessed him, not of doubt, which would have set him free, but of guile. The light broadened. Shinzo reached for the dipper. He had not emptied it once. Deliberately he rose and poured the water, but instead of counting the invocation he counted ten, stooping the while, that he might see the under side of the cloth. 'Ichi – ni – san – shi – go – roku – shichi – hachi – ku – ju.' In the pause the first drop globed itself and fell, with great deliberation. So had it done for seventeen days. Shinzo straightened himself. Then he went and searched in the brook for two rough stones, and when he had found them he stood over the Web of Expiation and ground the Sacred Name between them. He did it carefully, for it is not easy to hoodwink the gods. Then he filled the dipper and emptied it, uttering the words of invocation with great devotion and reverence. The fluff scraped from the cotton settled like fine clogging sand. He brushed it off with his hand and bent to look up. A spark of light gleamed in the opaque whiteness of the web, like the hole a child makes with a pin in the paper shutters. Shinzo laid down the dipper and went home to sleep, stepping carefully, for the dew was bright on the grass.

It happened when Shinzo was twenty-three. He is now middle-aged, and the father of seven sons. For in a few months time he married the sister of the wife of the Maker of Tubs, thereby performing his duty to the ancestors, and O Ba san died respecting him. But for himself he has no illusions. He knows that when he dies the devils will receive him and will grind him, even as he ground the sacred name of Buddha, between the upper and nether millstones of hell. Yet is his serenity unshaken. As he went home that morning, he saw O Tsuyu san reborn. She is a dewdrop in the lotus that grows before Kwannon in Paradise.

Notes

'Shinzo [Shinzō]': The handwritten copy has 'Sanjo', a name probably abandoned because of its royal associations noted previously, and because it is a family name. 'Shinzō' is an ordinary given name. This story of Shinzo, his childless wife, and his mother O Ba san, overlaps in many of its details with that in 'Kwannon of the Single Grace'.

'O Tsuyu san [*o*-Tsuyu-*san*]': This name does mean 'dew', as stated.

'the lacquer panels...': Isabella Bird describes these in her account of the temple at Asakusa, *Unbeaten Tracks in Japan: An Account of Travels in the Interior* (London: John Murray, 2nd edn ,1880), vol. I, p. 29.

'the Wheel': The cycle of reincarnation.

'tabako-bon [*tabako-bon*]': A small wooden box with a pot for ash and other things necessary to smoking. The pipe would have been a long thin one.

'O Shinzo': As elsewhere, the 'O' can be read as an apostrophe.

'tablet': This would have carried the posthumous Sanskrit name of the deceased.

'*Namu yo…*': More accurately, '*Namu Myōhô renge kyō*'; lit. 'I take refuge in the Lotus Sutra'. The invocation is correctly given by Isabella Bird, vol. I, p. 254.

'Nikko': There are temples in Nikkō, as everywhere, but they are subsidiary to the much more famous shrines.

'jinricksha-man': Rickshaw-man, as before.

'Ichi – ni – san… [*Ichi – ni – san…*]': The numbers one to ten.

Métier de Femme

When Yamato-Také, the Bamboo of Yamato, went against the barbarians of the east country, his wife went with him, and he took it ill. He was one of the eighty Princes of the Blood, and she was the Princess Oto-Tachibana, and her place was on the mats of the inner chamber. Yamato-Také was young – he was indeed only thirty-two when he died – and he was conservative with the intense conservatism of young men. Oto-Tachibana was beautiful. He would have chosen to return in the lull of his campaigns and find her the flower-soft creature he had left her, only that the Robe of the Plum Blossom would have changed with the season to the Robe of the Maple, and the sweetmeats which she would serve with the saké-cup, kneeling, would be maple-leaves scarlet and gold instead of cherry-blossom. Her long fingers were for the moulding and tinting of sweetmeats or the arranging of the iris on the daïs, or the writing of fragile verse. Yamato-Také was himself a writer of verses, composing a singularly exquisite quatrain as he lay dying on the Moor of Nobo, returned from his last great war. He was indeed a lover of all the Fine Arts, and of the beautiful, but especially in women. And Oto-Tachibana in the war garments disfigured herself. The small black cap confined the hair that should have rained on either side to her knees, and the white band came low on her forehead and marred the curve that was like the white fan of Fujisan, a thing to be desired in women. The war kimono was black with white lines of death upon it, and she followed him like his black shadow, instead of coming before his inward eye in robes that were the memory of grey dawn, or the mist of cherry blossom on the river, or the purple translucent shadows of the wisteria garden. He had not forbidden her; the devotion of a creature so exquisite could not but gratify him. None the less, she came on sufferance, nor was she allowed to forget it. Yamato-Také had a sense of the fitness of things; she found him as amorous as his sword-blade. It was as his page that she followed him, and his discipline was rigorous. Once when his coldness stung her to appeal, he laughed a little and bade her go home and await him upon the mats. So Oto-Tachibana followed him for the most part in silence, carrying his spear and shield, and was content when sometimes in the heat of the day he suffered her to take his head on her knee and shield him from the sun that was fast discolouring the ivory pallor of her face. If Yamato-Také had seen her then she was beautiful, for she took out the high jewelled comb that was the only relic of the old feminine luxury of the palace, and let her hair fall about him that it might shadow him, and Yamato-Také slept as soundly in the purple blackness as under the wistaria in the pond-arbour of the Palace garden. Only being asleep, Yamato-Také saw nothing.

So the march went on. Oto-Tachibana followed her lord, carrying his spear and shield. Her skin roughened and burned, till her face was like the faces of the peasant women they passed, working side by side with their husbands in the fields. There were hard places on her small palms with the friction of the spear; her lips were dry, and bitter with the dust of the road.

Moreover – Yamato-Také eyed it with disfavour – the kilted *hakama* suffered a freer step than the clinging crêpe folds of the court robes, and the necessity of keeping step with the men at arms was teaching Oto-Tachibana to stride. Now the woman's movement should be an undulation, nor should her foot pass beyond the circuit of white foam that is her garment's edge. It is an indecorum. It was the Prince himself who had checked her in the early days for delaying the line of march; nevertheless, he marked the freedom of her carriage, and distasted it. So they came beneath the shadow of the mountains, and there stayed.

It was the province of the Princes of Owari. Beyond the mountains lay the country of the eastern barbarians, a plain of fever and the hot Pacific winds. But here there was loyalty and peace. Every year the Daimyo of Owari made his progress to Yamato, to do homage to his lord the Emperor, though in late years the custom had been forgiven, since the hereditary right was vested in the person of the Princess Miyazu, a girl not yet given in marriage. Here, then, Yamato-Také halted to give his samurai a few days' breathing space, lodging the while in the yashiki where the Daimyos of Owari kept a state half royal. But when the days grew into weeks, the samurai marvelled openly; all but Oto-Tachibana. To her at least it was plain that her husband had found something beyond loyalty in the yashiki of the Princes of Owari.

They were received in the Hall of Audience: Yamato-Také standing alone, his samurai ranked in the lower part of the hall, his wife in the dusty war-garments a pace or two behind him, holding his spear and shield, and drooping a little in sheer lassitude of body and spirit. But when the screens on the daïs slid softly back, Oto-Tachibana strung herself, for the beauty of the Princess Miyazu challenged her like a blow. At the same moment Yamato-Také caught his breath, the little sharp intaking of the breath with which he greeted a perfect thing. Oto-Tachibana had heard it twice: once, at the 'Meeting of Eyes' before their betrothal, when she raised her head from her profound obeisance, and for the first time he saw her face; and again, at his first sight of the damascened blade by which the house of the Amakuni won their right to forge the Imperial Swords till the end of time.

The Princess Miyazu was moving slowly forward, again sinking in the reverence due to a Prince of the Empire. She was a lotus swaying in the palace moat when the water ripples with the leaping of a frog. Yamato-Také, starved of beauty, feasted. The whiteness of her face dazzled him. It was long since he had been startled by the scarlet of a woman's mouth. Mindful at last, he turned to where his wife still stood, grasping his spear and shield, and made as though to present her. But something checked him. Beside that other, Princess Oto-Tachibana looked like a woman of the fields. He could not own her. For that moment at least, he had no thought of treachery. Simply it irked him that the Princess Miyazu should have cause to think so little of his taste in women. As for the Princess, she saw the figure in the dusty war-garments, saw that Yamato-Také had brought a woman in his train. But her eyelids were the eyelids of discretion. She saw nothing.

They walked in the garden together, the Princess Miyazu and Yamato-Také. The Princess sent her ladies before her, and they shook the branches of the maple, and the old stone paths were a scarlet and gold brocade. She was alluring as a geisha, mannered as a great lady. Yamato-Také was fastidious and he found her absolute. They drank wine together; the Princess had a delicacy of palate marvellous in a woman, and the wine was good, and the design at the bottom of the saké cup so exquisite that one hasted to lay it bare again. They wrote verses, the Princess and her ladies, on Yamato-Také and the bamboo that was his namesake, the bamboo that is the most graceful of trees, the most terrible of war-spears, slender and smooth enough for the handle of a woman's fan. And Yamato-Také wrote verses, of hair that fell like the rain of willows, of a forehead adorable as Fuji, of hands that were melting snow, of a body young as herbs. All this Oto-Tachibana heard, for she waited upon him daily, poured the water upon his hands, spread the futons at night. Also, when at last the war fever broke again upon him, she heard him promise to return again that way, to take the Princess Miyazu to wife, and bring her in state to the Emperor his father at Yamato. Yet Oto-Tachibana said no word.

They took their journey from Owari, and came to where the mountains go down to the sea. There is no way by the sands. The samurai went hither and thither in the little fishing village of Sagami, bartering with the fishermen for boats, while Yamato-Také stood chafing on the beach, scowling across at the blue farther shore with the sea running strong and swift between. The name of the strait is Hashiri-mizu (Running Water), and

Yamato hearing it mocked and said, 'Running Water of a truth! A lad might jump it if he would.' Oto-Tachibana listening, saw the sparkling surface of the sea darken as if a cloud had passed over it. But when she looked, there was no cloud in the sky. She followed her husband on board his junk, but as she followed she was afraid.

They were about the middle of the strait when the storm burst. There was blackness and thunder and tempest and the sea was boiling pitch. The frail junk shuddered and plunged in a whirlpool where oar and rudder and sail were useless. Yamato-Také sat and looked sombrely before him, with the fear of the gods upon him and the thought of the cold strangling of water. Oto-Tachibana lay prone on her face and prayed, for with every lightning flash she saw the furious face of Rinjin, god of the sea, glaring at Yamato-Také, and in that distorted countenance there was no mercy. She fell again upon her face and prayed in an agony, but the first great wave broke over the side, and the timbers shuddered and strained. Then she rose, and knelt before Yamato-Také. 'Honourable One', she said softly, 'I have wherewith to appease the gods.' Yamato-Také gazed before him gloomily, and her words went past him as the words and the folly of women who will always be talking. So Oto-Tachibana went from him, and bade the samurai throw the mats of the sleeping-apartment into the sea; then turning again to her husband she cried as one who jests: 'In truth the woman's place is on the mats. Thou hast rightly said!' and at the unwonted sound of laughter in her voice he turned his head and looked, and saw her poised on the edge of the junk with the streams of her hair about her, for the storm had blown the war cap from her head, and the white curve of Fuji was again laid bare. Then she sprang. For a moment he saw her seated on the mats with her robes about her like a princess in the hall of audience, and then the darkness received her. There fell a great calm. The wind and the sea were quiet, and there was a silence like the silence of the deaf, and in the east the greyness of the dawn. It was white daylight when Yamato-Také and his samurai disembarked on the farther shore.

So, after all, Yamato-Také went against the barbarians alone. It was the fiercest and the longest of his wars, but it brought him great honour, and after many months he returned again. And at the summit of the mountain pass which is called the Usui Togi, he halted and looked down, and saw below him all the plain and the sea and the swift strip of blue water where she died. And standing there he cried three times '*Azuma waya! Azuma waya!*' which is 'Alas, my wife!' It is the name of Eastern Japan even now.

It was not her only memorial. For descending, the villagers brought him the jewelled comb that the sea had washed ashore on the seventh day, the comb that was her only ornament, and Yamato-Také built a great tomb over it and mourned there for her. Then after many days he departed again by the road that led to home, to bring tidings to the Emperor his father, and to see again Yamato,

'Yamato the most hidden of all lands'

— it is from the quatrain that he wrote before his death —

'Yamato, deep, buried in the hills.'

Nor was it his fault that the way to Yamato lies through the province of Owari.

Notes

'Bamboo of Yamato': *Take* is a word for bamboo in Japanese, but it does not mean that here. In this case it is an abbreviated form of *takeru*, meaning 'valiant' or 'brave', as Chamberlain's notes on the *Kojiki* make clear, (Introduction, note 71) p. 258. Yamato is the old name for the heartland of Japan in the west part of the country, before it expanded to the east.

'*hakama*': Divided skirts that are part of a man's formal attire, but in the middle ages were also sometimes worn by noble women.

'yashiki [*yashiki*]': Mansion, or large residence.

'wrote verses': The composition and exchange of complimentary verses, like many of the other elegant details and pursuits in this anachronistic tale, was a practice of the medieval court.

'Running Water': This detail, and the remainder of the story, more or less accurately follow the account in the *Kojiki*. See Chamberlain, pp. 261–5.

'name of Eastern Japan': *Azuma* means 'east' in modern Japanese; this still applies.

'Usui Togi [Usui-*tōge*]': The same pass that was adjacent to Karuizawa, where the Waddells went in summer.

'the quatrain that he wrote…': The original would not of course have been a quatrain, but a syllabic fragment. Compare the lines here with those in Chamberlain, p. 271. It is likely that Waddell took her model of the poem from Yone Noguchi, *The Spirit of Japanese Poetry* (London: John Murray, 1914), p. 78. However, her telling of the story is too detailed to have been drawn from Noguchi's brief account, and must have come from Chamberlain directly. See also the Appendix.

PART 3:

The Uttermost Isles:
Essays on Literature

THE UTTERMOST ISLES

By HELEN WADDELL

Illustrations by S. Ichikawa

Then she said to the mother of Hasan, the mourning, the wretched, "O my mistress, thou wilt render me desolate by thine absence. But when thy son hath come, and the days of separation have become tedious to him, and he desireth approach and meeting, and the winds of love and longing desire agitate him, let him come to me in the Islands of Wak-wak." And she flew away with her children and sought her country.

THE Thousand and One Nights are a little sultry: this is the only sentence through which the wind blows. But then the story of Hasan of El Basrah, by so much the greatest and most neglected romance of them all, was born of the desert and the sea. It is Arabian, not Persian. There is no scattering of perfumes in it, no buying of Othmanee quinces and peaches of Oman, jasmine ...

the challenge of Menar-es-Sena to the Islands whose name is like the crying of wild birds. Lane has a footnote to the effect that the Islands of Wak-wak are to be identified with Sarawak in Borneo. But it is better to listen to 'Abd-el Kuddoos, the paternal uncle of the eldest damsel of the Palace of the Mountain on whose top the clouds divide: "O my son, relinquish this most vexatious affair. For thou couldst not gain access to the Islands of Wak-wak even if the Flying Jinn and the wandering stars assisted thee, since between thee and those Islands are seven valleys and seven mountains of vast magnitude." Or to the Sheykh Abu-r-Ruweysh who said to his fellow scholars, each of them seated on a divan before a perfuming vessel containing fire and incense, while students read aloud to them their own works, "O my brothers, verily this is a great and perilous affair, and I have not seen any hate life except this young man." For the creator of Hasan is one of the great enchanters: and his Islands to which one travels through "valleys and thirsty lands and fatal places" are

Born of sad love and unfulfilled desire.

Yet not the uttermost isles. For these, one goes farther east and farther west. For Hasan came ...

...rned and went slowly from the place.

"There is no help in me," said Yusai, when he had found him. "It is the blind man who is wise in the dark. But there is Ryoseki, high-priest of ...in Banzui-In. I know him, and will give you letters to him." It was dark in the temple courts when Hagiwara again passed under the great gateway. He stood silently by while Ryoseki read the letter in which Yusai had told his story for him, watching the light of the *andon* shining on his shaven crown. There was no change on the unmoved face: it seemed to look on the writhing brood of human desires, remote as the quiet Buddha in the shadows behind him. At last he raised his head, and looked on the young distraught countenance before him: the desire of the dead was an old story to him: he had heard it many times. "It is death

BEFORE THE TOMB A SCARLET LANTERN HUNG:

IT WAS A SILK LANTERN, WITH A GAY BUNCH OF PEONIES DROOPING FROM THE HANDLE

and not to Hagiwara. Rousing Tomozo from his sleep, she bound him with curses so terrible and so potent a fear that the old man swore to do her bidding. And when the darkness fell again, and Tomozo spread his master's *futon* on the floor, a single scroll was gone from the lattice above his head, and the image of the Buddha had been slipped from the folds of his girdle. Worn out and over watched, Hagiwara flung himself down, and the invocation of the Buddha died on his drowsy lips. Before midnight he was sound, so sound that when the light of the peony lantern fell on his face, he stirred and held out his arms without waking from his sleep. In the morning they found him dead, with that which had been the body of O-Tsuyu-san beside him. At his feet stood the peony lantern: it had gone out.

The original printing of 'The Uttermost Isles' with illustrations.

The Hyacinth Fields

It was some time in the fourth century that T'ao Yüan Ming wrote the Chinese variant of the legend of the Before Time, which the world has been telling itself since the evening and the morning were the second day. It is the story of a fisherman of Wu-ling; how he one day fished farther up the river than was his wont, and beyond a bend in the stream came upon a valley of peach trees in blossom; how the valley stretched far into the mountains and he followed it, and came down upon the farther side into a great and quiet land, with green fields, and young and old working in them. Their clothes were strange to him, but their words, when he spoke to them, were like his own, though of an older accent. For they were of his province, these, but had come from it many generations since, fleeing from the evil of the House of Ch'in. No trouble had since befallen them; of the rise of the Han dynasty they knew nothing, and they sorrowed with him over the chances of the world. For a long time they entertained him in their houses, and he was sorry when he had to go from them, and took many notes of the way, that he might come again. 'It will not be worth while to speak of us', they said courteously, when he took leave of them; but he thought otherwise, acquainting no less a person than the Governor.

The Governor sent officials of State to accompany him on his return, that they might report upon that happy valley; yet, though the fisherman studied his notes never so carefully, he was not able to bring them there. The bend in the river always eluded him; he never could find it again.

And this is fortunate. For that undiscovered bend is responsible for most literature. Greece, not a very Attic Greece, lay behind it for the Elizabethans. The eighteenth century glimpsed the Middle Ages there, and remoter reaches still, which they set out to find with the notes of that very untrustworthy fisherman, James Macpherson. Curiously, the Seeker in time becomes the Sought. Keats heard the Elizabethan drinking choruses come faintly down the stream. Malory followed 'the French Coke', and himself became for the nineteenth century the complete angler. Of late, the impression is that we have sufficiently fished those upper reaches; nothing less than a whole new river will content us, with the continent of Asia round the bend. There is a little initial difficulty in the matter of portages, but this the Orientalists, the scholars, do for us; draymen, very porters: behold us launched. 'Having discovered Chinese painting', they tell us, 'we are slowly beginning to discover Chinese poetry'; and discovering Chinese poetry, will find salvation. The Rubáiyát has not saved us: Japanese art did not give us its liquid line: but Chinese poetry has the simple efficacy of a revelation in religion. The reed pipe is to shame us from our virtuosity; our poets are to strip off their singing robes, to sing, in fact, in their working clothes. They are not even to sing, they are to say. For Chinese poetry, 'the poetry of tomorrow', is 'more reasonable' than ours, 'nearer prose'.

Now this kind of language serves a little to rouse that part which Hasan of El Basrah has in all of us when he says, 'There is no country better than my country, and everything in it is better than what there is in all the other countries, and its people are good people, with comely faces'. One submits that lyrics of Donne's – and heaven knows Donne was without carefulness – 'happen' to us as surely as if they had been translated from the Chinese; that Po Chü-i may draw a more beguiling melody from his Chinese penny whistle than all our dexterity from the violin, yet will the violin remain the nobler instrument; and that if it comes to penny whistles, Blake was no mean performer thereon. That, to be plain with you, Abana and Pharpar, rivers of Damascus, are better than this Jordan, and we will continue washing in them, which is to be not a little ungracious.

Foolish, also. For every bend in the river is a grateful thing to us who are for ever threatened with the canal. And the idea of the bend is surely the peculiar property of the East. The tenth of a farthing will buy it for you in the Tokio streets, all infinity in the circuit of a fan; the unseen bay between two pine-fringed headlands, the single headland beyond which lie you know not what 'fair cities and delicate coasts'. All Japanese sea-coasts stretch to infinity. This, too, is the reason why so many of their fairy-tales are a little grey and mournful in their endings. For there is no finality in an unhappy ending; it postulates an eternity, in which all these sorrowful things shall be made up. There is less infinity of reach in their verse; yet one remembers *tankas*, translated by Yone Noguchi, that have the sudden depth of wells. The first of them is a mother's lament for her little son: –

'The hunter of dragonflies,
To-day how far away
May he have gone!'

The second should be written in the grass character on a scroll, and hung in the low-browed inn on the Usui Pass that looks across a sea of mountains to Fuji itself –

'Being tired,
Ah, the time I fall into the inn,
– The wisteria flowers!'

There is a world between them: yet in one thing they are alike, that they have each captured the moment, blotted out past and future into the eternal Now, which is the perpetual mood of deity: certainly the test of divinity in lyric poets.

Moreover, for our peculiar need, it may well be that the untroubled reaches of these Chinese waters are more nearly answerable. For thirty years we have thirsted for the cooling draught of the Augustan peace; yet one suspects that the waters of Bath and Tunbridge Wells are too medicated for the disease of our self-consciousness. The eighteenth century is not primary enough: its admirable manner is 'that controlled self-consciousness which is the expensive substitute for simplicity.' And China, the China of Mr. Waley's poets and Professor Giles's biographies, is the eighteenth century, but an eighteenth century that has entered the kingdom of heaven and become a little child. With a great sum the Augustans obtained their freedom: these were free-born.

The eighteenth century was not civilised enough to be simple: they dare not obey Dryden's 'Trust nature: do not labour to be dull'. Chinese civilisation is a thing so old that itself is a natural object,

> 'Rolled round in earth's diurnal course
> With rocks and stones and trees.'

The Augustans are a little like the actors of the Elizabethan stage: magnificently habited, with a background of bare boards. The Chinese background is an immemorial setting of ceremony of state and landscape gardens. It projects itself even upon eternity. To Li Ho, having finished his term on earth, came a green man riding on a hornless dragon, and said, 'God Almighty has finished building his Jade Pavilion, and desireth you to be his secretary'. They all enjoy 'their comfortable importances', these men of letters, the while they call themselves the Idlers of the Bamboo Brook. It is the blend of massive dignity with a sort of childlike directness in living that is their charm. Ku K'ai-chih is one of the Four Masters in Chinese art: but they remember him most happily for his way of eating sugar cane, beginning at the wrong end, and 'passing gradually', as he himself expressed it, 'into Paradise'. Life seems to have come to them naturally as that true poem which Milton – that mortal part of Milton which was so much more Augustan than Jacobean – strove so disastrously to make his own; except that Aubrey says he always had a garden where he lived. There is no imagining these Chinese *littérateurs* without their gardens: Ts'ui Li-Chih, magistrate, who spent his time reciting verses under the pine trees in his courtyard, and who, when anyone came to see him, courteously replied, 'I am engaged in official business; please excuse me'. Fu Pu-Ch'i, sitting in his judgement hall and playing on the lute, while five inhabitants, more virtuous than he, administered his province: 'You put your trust in energy', he said to a more active colleague, 'I in men; mine is the better method'. Liu Ling, to whom, peaceably drinking in his pavilion, two neighbours came to reason of temperance and judgement; whereupon Liu Ling, having provided himself with a fresh flagon, sat down, and by alternately sipping and stroking his beard, lulled himself into that state when, as he said to himself, 'eternity seems but a single day'. 'So he sat' – for Liu Ling has a pleasant habit of referring to himself as 'an elderly gentleman of my acquaintance' – 'his ears were beyond the reach of thunder: he could not have seen a mountain. Heat and cold existed for him no more. He knew not even the workings of his own mind. To him the affairs of this world appeared but as so much duckweed in a river, while the two philanthropists agitated at his side like two wasps trying to convert a caterpillar.'

To come upon writing like this is to begin to understand the primary quality of the Chinese mind. One ceases to wonder that the characters of their alphabet, so much older than ours, are still young; still sketches in black and white, and each of them symbolic. Our sounds once meant something to us, and now and then a fragment of a line of Keats reminds us how many fair and fragile things begin with the letter *f*. But for the most part sounds must crowd into words, and words to sentences, and sentences to paragraphs, to take effect on our insensitiveness. So, too, with the giving of names, which is the art of painting in little. There are a score of them scattered through the 'Chinese Biographical Dictionary', and every one of them a scene upon a fan. There is the ascetic Marquis of Yeh, whom the countryside eternalised as the Immortal Collarbone; Yen Ts'an, so glorious in his potations that they called him the Drunken Dragon; Hsiao Man, the Willow Wand, mistress of the poet Po Chü-i, whose beauty lingers in the wine flagon that is her namesake, because the line of it recalled the far-famed curve of her waist; Ch'ao Fei-yen, the Flying Swallow, seen dancing one night by the Emperor Ch'eng Ti when he wandered the streets in disguise; Han Fu, the Red Flicker, from the colour and gesture of her fan: lyrics in little; dead butterflies staining the sober pages with the dust of their vivid wings. They still have the art of the significant gesture in China. There is one story Rabelais would have loved, of the wealthy branch of the Yüan family who on the seventh day of the seventh moon spread out their fur robes and costly robes of ceremony for airing, as is the custom in China: while the Bohemian nephew living in art and poverty across the way hangs out a solitary pair of trousers, explaining to his friends that he is a victim to the tyranny of custom. They are forever making pictures; though not all on the scale of that Emperor, lover of P'an Fei, who had lilies carved on the soles of her small shoes, and the streets strewn with gold leaf when she passed, that flowers might indeed spring up behind her. There is too much composition in that picture: the Chinese method is nearer the spirit of their own proverb, 'The peach and the plum tree speak not, yet around them are seen the footprints of men'. And perhaps the most characteristic story of all is of that general Liu Kun who defended Chin-Yang against the Tartars, some time in the fourth century. The city was straitly sieged and hope all but gone, when one moonlight night the general climbed the tower and there played wandering airs upon the Tartar pipe. The barbarians stood in the door of their tents and heard him, sick for home; and in the morning the plain was empty and the great hordes gone.

Even so, the reed pipe has begun to play for more remote barbarians. And one remembers a fairy tale that is also, since it was written in the actual eighteenth century, something of a parable: the story of a student in Peking who had finished his course, and wandered into the Temple of Mysteries, before he should go back to his home in the provinces. There, he came upon a wall-painting in an unfrequented corridor, a troop of goddesses gathering hyacinths in a meadow: but one of the goddesses was younger than the rest, for her hair was still low on her neck, and looking upon her, this student loved her. He knelt before the painting for a long time, perhaps passing into a trance. For it seemed to him that the youngest of the goddesses stepped out of the wall-painting, and down the corridor and through the courtyard to her own chamber. The student followed her, and had but knelt at her feet to crave her kindness when there came a trampling of feet upon the stone. Terrified, she hid him behind a screen, and a great god in armour with a black lacquer face came through the door. He questioned, she protested: at last he went, ill satisfied, taking the youngest of the goddesses with him. When the student came to himself, he was still kneeling before the wall-painting. Yet something had happened. For the goddess with her hair low on her neck was no longer in the hyacinth meadow. 'Where is she?' he cried to a passing priest, and the priest looked upon him, kindly. 'Go home, young man', he said. 'She is waiting for you in your own village.'

Notes

'T'ao Yüan Ming': Also known as T'ao Chien (AD 365–427). Herbert A. Giles interprets the tale thus, in a book that Waddell may have drawn on: 'The gods had permitted the poet to go back for a brief span to the peach-blossom days of his youth.' *A History of Chinese Literature* (London: William Heinemann, 1901), p. 131. Chinese names are given in roman letters according to the orthography of the time, without attempting to modernise this.

'"French Coke"': The indication is uncertain; the typed version has 'Soke'.

'*tankas* [*tanka*]': In fact these verses are not tanka, but haiku (which at that time were still called *hokku* or *haikai*). The first was traditionally ascribed to the nun Chiyo (1703–75), and was thought to be about her infant son, but modern scholarship doubts the ascription. The second verse is a well-known one by Matsuo Bashō (1644–94), the greatest of these poets.

'Rolled round ... ': The concluding lines of Wordsworth's short lyric 'A slumber did my spirit seal'. See William Wordsworth, *The Poems*, vol. I, ed John O. Hayden (Harmondsworth: Penguin, 1982) p. 364.

'Mr. Waley's poets': Arthur Waley's first volume of translations had been published recently by Constable, the same publisher that issued Waddell's own *Lyrics from the Chinese*. She reviewed Waley several times. See the Introduction, pp. 47–8.

'Professor Giles's biographies': Waddell draws extensively on Herbert A. Giles's two-volume *Chinese Biographical Dictionary* (London: Bernard Quaritch/Shanghai and Yokohama: Kelly and Walsh, 1898), as she acknowledges herself. Her use of this work is highly selective, and a few of the details are confused.

'primary quality': Waddell's view was supported not only by the works of Giles, but also by those of James Legge, from whom she had drawn most of her own Chinese lyrics. See the *She King, or Book of Poetry*, translated by Legge as the fourth volume of his *Chinese Classics* (Taipei: SMC Publishing 1991; first published Hong Kong, 1871).

'fairy tale': The source of this story has not yet come to light.

The Uttermost Isles

Then she said to the mother of Hasan, the mourning, the wretched. 'O my mistress, thou wilt render me desolate by thine absence: but when thy son hath come, and the days of separation have become tedious to him and he desireth approach and meeting, and the winds of love and longing desire agitate him, let him come to me in the Islands of Wak-wak.' And she flew away with her children and sought her country.

The Thousand and One Nights are a little sultry: this is the only sentence through which the wind blows. But then the story of Hasan of El Basrah, by so much the greatest and most neglected romance of them all, was born of the desert and the sea. It is Arabian, not Persian; there is no scattering of perfumes in it, no buying of Othmanee quinces and peaches of Oman, jasmine of Aleppo and water-lilies of Damascus. But there is sea-light, a sea blue and foaming, and a 'long coast' of pebbles, white and yellow and blue and black, more convincing than Sinbad's sea-coasts. One suspects Sinbad's roaring sea: it is too consistently agitated with waves. And there is a vast blue mountain of which even the stones were blue, and in it a cavern with a door of iron from China: a ride through the desert on a steed 'swifter than the blinding lightning,' with all the wild horses of the desert racing beside him, 'numerous as drops of rain'; and a flight on the shoulders of the 'Efreet, Dahnash the Flyer, 'who rose with him to the clouds of heaven and proceeded with him a day and a night till he heard the praises of the Angels in heaven: and when the dawn came he put him down on a land white like camphor, and departed'. But the finest invention is the half-lyrical fragment with which the slow rhythmic movement of the prose is haunted. Its creator never wearies of it: whenever Hasan pauses in his wanderings to tell his tale anew – and in the manner of the *Arabian Nights* he tells it many times – his story ends with the challenge of Menar-es-Sena to the Islands whose name is like the crying of wild birds. Lane has a footnote to the effect that the Islands of Wak-wak are to be identified with Sarawak in Borneo: but it is better to listen to 'Abd-el-Kuddoos, the paternal uncle of the eldest damsel of the Palace of the Mountain on whose top the clouds divide: 'O my son, relinquish this most vexatious affair: for thou couldst not gain access to the Islands of Wak-wak even if the Flying Jinn and the wandering stars assisted thee, since between thee and those Islands are seven valleys [and seven seas] and seven mountains of vast magnitude', or to the Sheykh Abu-r-Ruweysh who said to his fellow scholars, each of them seated on a divan before a perfuming vessel containing fire and incense, while students read aloud to them their own works, 'O my brothers, verily this is a great and perilous affair, and I have not seen any hate life, except this young man'. For the creator of Hasan [of El Basrah] is one of the great enchanters: and his Islands to which one travels through 'valleys and thirsty lands and fatal places' are

Born of old love and unfulfilled desire.

Yet not the uttermost isles. For these, one goes farther east and farther west. For Hasan came back with Menar-es-Sena from the Islands of Wak-wak [, came back] to Bagdad the Abode of Peace, entering his house by the private door which opened to the desert and the plain: and there they ceased not to pass the most comfortable life and the most agreeable, until they were visited by the Terminator of Delights and the Separator of Companions. It is the end of all things for the story-teller: his hearers acquiesce. There is passion in the *Arabian Nights*, once or twice passion transcendent; but it does not go beyond the Even Pass of Yomi, which is the halting place between the living and the dead. 'Mourn not for thy wife', said Sinbad. 'God will happily compensate thee by giving thee one better than she, and thy life will be long if it be the will of God, whose name be exalted!' There are seven valleys and seven seas and seven mountains of vast magnitude between that and Heine's

Mein süsses Lieb, wenn du im Grab,
Im dunkeln Grab wirst liegen,

or the fragment from the Odes of the Royal Domain,

Living, we lie asunder.
Dead, we shall share one grave.

'"Know" said the king, "that this is the custom in our country, when the husband dieth, we bury with him his wife, and when the wife dieth, we bury with her her husband: that we may not separate them in life or in death." "By Allah", said Sinbad, "this custom is exceeding vile."'; wherein, outsider as he is even in the *Arabian Nights*, he voiced the sentiment of the waking half of literature.

But the dream-half: in Lafcadio Hearn's translations of Japanese folk song;

Even the knot of rope tying our boats together
Knotted was long ago by some love in a former birth.

So that we stay together, even the hell of the Blood Lake,
Even the Mountain of Swords, will signify nothing at all:

in the *Koh Sang* of the Odes of T'ang;

Through the long nights of winter,
Through the long days of summer I abide alone,
Till the lapse of a hundred years,
When I shall go home to his chamber:

in Donne's *Relique* and *Nocturnal*; in Heine's

Wir beide bleiben in der Gruft,
Ich liege in deinem Arme.

The sum of it is in the greatest of all legends, the [dream and the awaking that makes a] single line of Milton one of the marvels of the world:

His half-regained Eurydice.

Strange that to him of all men was this grace given, to capture for once the bitter of the sweet.

For it is the most bitter sweet of all dreams, this of the restoring of the dead: the core of fire that makes luminous the burial rites of the Egyptians: the grain [undying] in the mummy's hand. 'Women received their dead raised to life again: and others were tortured, not accepting deliverance, that they might obtain a better resurrection'; one remembers one's childish pondering over the strange refusal of the intimate sure sweetness of return to this world of sunlight and trees. And even yet, it is 'to the sentiment of the body, the flesh of whose force and colour that wandering Platonic soul was so frail an abstract', that we cling. Flesh and blood cannot inherit the Kingdom of God; but the craving that it might be so still shelters in the wording of the Creed. St. Paul fought it, his metaphors breaking and straining with too much way, sublimating the flesh by the intolerable radiance of the spirit: 'mortality swallowed up of life'. Buddhism fought it, with less transcendent weapon[s]: 'neither doth corruption inherit incorruption'. It is death, not in its priest-like task of cold ablution, but death the revealer of the secret taint, the sickening flavour of mortality, that veins the illusion of the sensuous world. 'Spirit must brand the flesh, that it may live.'

We deceive ourselves better in the West than in the East. Persephone comes back with no shadow on her face. Clarimonde, carrying the small sepulchral lamp that is left in tombs, is unchanged, only for the fainter scarlet of her smile, and the withering of the blue flowers in her hair. Orpheus saw Eurydice before she sank back into darkness, and that recognition has become one of our symbols for the infinite [hunger]. That is why the Japanese version of the legend, earth-stained and cavern-lighted, seems at first a horrible thing: and it is a long time before one sees the beauty in the horror.

* * *

They were the seventh of the divine generations, Izanagi and Izanami, the mortal gods of whom the Immortals were begotten. They stood together on the Floating Bridge of Heaven, and Izanagi plunged the Jewel-spear into the green swirl of the sea. Drops of brine fell from it, and they saw an island born. Together they went down to see the land that they had made, and parted, going their different ways upon it: and when they met again, each found the other fair. There were no men in the Land of the Reed Plains, which is now Japan, nor any gods but their two selves, and there they lived together. All the islands of the Inland Sea were of their making: until the day that Izanami brought the God of Burning Fire to birth, and died of the anguish. Then Izanagi wept for her, saying, 'O Thine Augustness, my lovely younger sister! That I should have exchanged thee for this single child!' and drawing his sword he slew the child, and took up his wife and buried her. But he was not comforted; and after some days he rose and went to seek her in the Land of Yomi, which is the country of the Dead. She saw him coming, and raising the door of the Palace she stood within the shadows while he cried to her, 'Thine Augustness, my lovely younger sister, the lands that thou and I made are not yet finished making: wherefore come back'. But she made answer, 'Alas that thou didst delay thy coming! I have eaten of the furnace of Yomi. But I would fain go back. Wait for me, while I plead with the Gods of Yomi. And look not upon me.' For a long time he waited: but she was long of coming. And when he could no longer endure the hunger of his desire, he lit a torch and crossed the threshold to find her. She lay within the threshold and she had seen corruption.

Then he turned and fled. And she rose, crying out at the shame he had put upon her, and followed him. But at the Even Pass of Yomi he hurled a great rock upon the path, and they stood, he on this side, and she on that, and took leave of one another. And she said, 'My lovely elder brother, Thine Augustness, for this I will in one day strangle to death a thousand of the people of thy land'. And he made answer, 'My lovely younger sister, Thine Augustness, for this I will in one day set up a thousand and five hundred houses of birth in my land, so that the living shall be more than the dead'. So they parted, and she returned and became the Goddess of the Land of Yomi. But for himself he came out upon the clover fields in the island of Tsukushi, which of all the islands lies over against the sun. And he cried aloud 'Oh hideous! I am come from a hideous and polluted land', and plunged into the river to purify himself. And from the waters of purification the gods were born.

* * *

It is the oldest Japanese legend: that shrinking from corruption is part of the elemental fastidiousness of the race. Buddhism only intensified it: bound up with it its own mistrust of love as the fleshliest of the lusts that bind the soul to the senses. It is hard at best for a man to see the world as a mirage flung upon eternity, to let its affairs go past him like cloud rack, 'indistinct, as water is in water'. But when love comes upon him, and all the sweetness of the world becomes incarnate in one 'small but ravishing substance' – 'nothing else is'.

There is no lantern can lighten
The dusk of the way of love,

says a Buddhist proverb: and the story of the Botan-Doro is the story of the Peony Lantern that lighted one fool the way to death.

It is the Japanese contemporary of *La Morte Amoureuse*: written in the last century, and on the same theme, the love that binds the living and the dead. But there the likeness ends. For Gautier's city lies always under the shadow of a cloud: and the 'insubstantial pageant' of the love between the priest and his dead mistress is the stuff of dreams; the one reality is her beauty, and it shines through a twilight of green water. Encho's city is Tokyo at the end of the eighteenth century, with daylight on its streets. There is a brawl between *samurai* before a sword-smith's shop in Hongo, and Encho, great master of the colloquial as he is, records the ecstatic comments of the crowd with an affectionate detachment, a little like Chaucer's. There is no heightening of the style: no attempt at intensity: the story ends in terror, but it is the slow terror that grows in sunlight; a worse thing to those who know it than any terror by night.

Two things change not since the Age of the Gods:
The flowing of water, the coming of Love.

It is as idyllic an opening as the meeting of Troilus and Cressida in the orchard: a scene that has never had its due. Only for Cressida's sophisticated white-foxglove beauty, there is O-Tsuyu-san, Dew of the Morning, as perishable and fair as the purple flower of the convolvulus; and for Troilus, Hagiwara the *samurai*, one and twenty, 'handsome to the pitch of making one think what a beautiful woman he would have made', and rather more of a scholar than a *samurai* should be. Pandarus had routed him from his books to see the plum blossoms at Kameido, and on their way from the great temple, a little flown with beauty and cold saké, suggested a private view of the plum trees in the garden of his old friend Iijima Heizaemon. For Iijima, who at two and twenty killed his man in the brawl with which the novel begins, is now a middle aged *samurai*, inheritor of the paternal estates, married for the second time, and something harassed in consequence. O-Tsuyu-san was too fair for the young wife: and so it came that her seventeenth year found her solitary mistress of her father's garden-villa in the suburb of the Hill of the Willows, with her maid O-Yoné to wait upon her. It is not customary in Japan for a woman to be from under authority. 'And this it was', says Encho, who is something of the mediaeval moralist, 'which was the beginning of the downfall of the house of Iijima'.

Yet Pandarus was a guileless Pandarus: the old family physician of both their houses, pleasantly facetious, fond of 'the ladies' – even in Japan one says the ladies – and given to the improvising of verses. He improvised several as they strolled on the stone paths, guided by O-Yoné;

Plum-trees in blossom!
What a background
For lighting one's pipe —

Hagiwara lingering just a little, for behind the sliding screens he saw the flowing of a faint purple sleeve. Thereafter they sat on the mats in the place of honour, while O-Yoné waited upon them with tea and sweetmeats. Her young mistress sat in the shadow, her long sleeves sweeping to the floor: after the first inaudible welcome to the stranger *samurai*, she had not opened her lips. Hagiwara too sat silent, his eyes fixed on her face. O-Yoné and the old physician had much to say to each other: the waiting woman of fiction does not alter with race or generation: and above and below the flying shuttle of their wit the web of the Great Illusion wove about these two. The afternoon light on the paper shutters behind O-Tsuyu faded: the faint purple of her dress grew grey. The guests rose: O-Yoné lighted lanterns, and passed with the old man to the entrance way. For a moment the two were left alone.

'I shall come back', said Hagiwara, stumbling in his speech. O-Tsuyu-san shivered and stirred.

'If you do not come back', she said, 'I shall die'.

Now if O-Tsuyu-san had been a *geisha*, her story would have been the sorry little tragi-comedy that is the life of most *geisha*. But she was of the house of a *samurai*, and, by her mother's side, of the *hatamoto*, the proudest of them all. That Hagiwara should return alone would be to outrage an immemorial etiquette: and the old physician was no fool. Already he was regretting his weakness for seeing the young people enjoying themselves; and Hagiwara's importunities for a second visit found him supple and evasive. Hagiwara chafed and sulked at the vexatious delays of age: the old man meditated the finding of an official go-between for both their houses: and while he pondered, O-Tsuyu-san fell strangely ill. There is an eighteenth century *hokku* of lament for the noon-convolvulus, born when the sun is fiercest, beyond succour of the morning or evening dews. It might have been written for her. 'Love that availeth more than you or I' was too fierce a passion for anything so fragile. She died, withered by its heat.

Months after, Hagiwara sat solitary in his house. It was the thirteenth night of the seventh moon; the night of the Feast of the Bon. All over the darkening streets lanterns were lighted to guide the returning dead. Hagiwara had lighted his lantern, but as he hung it above his threshold his heart named one name only. He had written it in his fine scholar's hand on the white tablets of the dead: had set wine and flowers below it: and now he sat and dreamed in the silence of the July night. Never, it seemed to him, had he so known solitude. For in April and May the spring nights had yearned with him for her: in June the rains dripping from the eaves and running mournfully in the leaden gutters had wept for her. But in July the earth is at rest and quiet: it is the stillness of satisfied desire. By August the glory is a little tarnished: in September it quickens toward[s] a diviner thing. But July has the fulness of possession, and the nights are of quiet breath. Once the tinkle of a *samisen* drifted across the bamboo fence: *geisha* returning late. It was a plaintive little song, but a laughing voice that sang it.

Three years thought of her,
Five years sought her,
Only for one night held her in my arms.

'Not for one night', said Hagiwara.

– And never twice in a single birth the same night comes.

There was no sound for a long time after the tinkling of the *samisen* passed by. The house was a lonely house, and out of the track of wayfarers.

A haze drifted across the moon, and after that the night seemed yet more still. Hagiwara stepped down from his verandah, and paced the glimmering garden. Suddenly from very far off, he heard the faint musical clink of women's *geta*. The sound came nearer; they were in the lane beyond the bamboo fence. Hagiwara went swiftly to the wicket in the bamboo, his silk *hakama* rustling as he strode, and opening it, stood in the shadow. Two women came through the dusk, one gaily dressed, holding a silken lantern, with a bunch of scarlet peonies drooping from the handle: the slighter figure behind her he could not well see, but she wore the long sleeves of rank, and her shadowy robes fell about her like the flower of the purple convolvulus. Hagiwara made a step forward.

'O-Yoné!' he cried.

The girl raised the lantern so that the light fell upon his face.

'Hagiwara-*sama*! And they told my mistress you were dead'. 'It was she they told me was dead', said Hagiwara: the slender figure in the shadow had not stirred. 'And your house was shuttered and empty'.

'They took us from it', said O-Yoné, 'and we found a small house in the Yanaka-no-Sasaki. It is a narrow house: there is only room for our two selves. And it is hard for us to live. My mistress is pale and thin.'

Then Hagiwara held out his hands to them and drew them in. But as his mistress passed him, she shrank a little, and hid her face in her long sleeve. 'Sir', she said, 'I have no beauty now'. In a passion of pity he caught her and swept the sleeve from her face. O-Yoné raised the lantern, so that the glow from it fell upon her. And when he saw her, his strength went from him, for he had not remembered that she was so fair.

It was near the dawn when they left him, stepping across the grey dews. That night they came again, and the night after, and for many nights, still lighted by the peony lantern. All day Hagiwara went restlessly to and fro; the lines of his face grew sharpened, and there was a sleepless light in his eyes. Tomozo, the old retainer who slept in the courtyard, watched him sorrowfully: night after night he saw the lamp burn late: was it for a *samurai* to sit so late at his books? On the eighth night he rose from his bed, to plead with him. His hand was on the sliding screen when he was startled by a sound: his master's low contented laugh. Much learning had indeed made him mad. Tomozo stooped and peered through the slit in the screens. His master lay under the mosquito net, pillowed on a woman's arm. Her face was bent over him: but as Tomozo gazed she lifted her head and he saw it. It was the face of a woman a great while dead.

Now Hagiwara had a friend, the great scholar Hakuodo Yusai. He too had pondered over his changed looks: and when he awakened in the moonlight to find Tomozo clawing his lattice-shutters with shaking hands and trembling in an ague, he had the old man in and heard his story to the end. In the morning he came himself to Hagiwara. Once again he listened, though to a different story.

'And your mistress – where is her honourable dwelling?' he asked politely.

'I do not know', said Hagiwara, taken aback. 'Only that it is in the quarter of Yanaka-no-Sasaki.'

'It is a large quarter', said Yusai; and at the irony of it Hagiwara flung from the house. All that day he went up and down Yanaka-no-Sasaki: it is a poor quarter; there are many houses and the streets are dim. But in none was any trace of O-Tsuyu, nor her maid O-Yoné. Reluctant and very sore, he turned to go home: and it chanced that his way led him through the temple grounds of Shin-Banzui-In. It was twilight, and the grey peace of the graves was grateful to him. His anger fell away from him; and when he saw down one of the aisles the scarlet glimmer of a lantern, his heart leaped, for surely it was she. He would make haste to overtake her, and upbraid her for lingering so late in that solitary place. He reached it: it was indeed solitary. Two graves were there: one a tomb of fresh-cut stone, with wealthy offerings before it: the other a little grave, neglected and poor. Before the tomb a scarlet lantern hung: it was a silk lantern, with a gay bunch of peonies drooping from the handle. Hagiwara stood a long time looking at it.

There came a patter of quick feet behind him, and he roused himself and turned: it was a small belated acolyte hurrying to reach the temple before the great bell boomed. He caught the boy and questioned him.

'It is the tomb of O-Tsuyu-san, daughter of Iijima Heizaemon', said the boy. 'She died young. That is O-Yoné her maid beside her. They say she would not live after her.' The sound of his flying sandals echoed behind him. Hagiwara stood, still gazing at the peony lantern. He knew now. Had he not always known? 'They took us from our house…we found a small house in the Yanaka-no-Sasaki. It is a narrow house: there is only room for our two selves. And it is hard for us to live. My mistress is pale and thin.' He turned and went slowly from the place.

'There is no help in me', said Yusai, when he had found him. 'It is the blind man who is wise in the dark. But there is Ryoseki, high-priest of Shin-Banzui-In. I know him, and will give you letters to him.' It was dark in the temple courts when Hagiwara again passed under the great gateway. He stood silently by while Ryoseki read the letter in which Yusai had told his story for him, watching the light of the *andon* shining on his shaven crown. There was no change on the unmoved face: it seemed to look on the writhing brood of human desires, remote as the quiet Buddha in the shadows behind him. At last he raised his head, and looked on the young distraught countenance before him; the desire of the dead was an old story to him: he had heard it many times. 'It is death for the body and damna-

From *In Ghostly Japan* by Hearn.

tion for the soul', he said. 'Wherefore take these. Paste the sacred scrolls over every lattice in your house, that no evil thing may enter it. This image of the Buddha, wear it in the folds of your girdle, and the dead will have no power on your body. And in the hour of your temptation recite the holy sutras, that you may keep your soul.'

As the priest counselled, it was done. Through the long hours Hagiwara knelt, reciting the Treasure-Sutra for which the Buddha offered his life to the Evil One. The night dragged slowly. At last, very far off, the sound of women's *geta* struck upon his ear. Above the sound of his chanting he heard it coming near. It stopped; the paper shutters turned rosy in a sudden glow; and above the name of the Buddha he heard her call his own. The chant died on his lips. Again she called him; he heard her small hands struggling with the shutters, and it was as though they struggled with his heart. She touched the sacred scroll: there was a terrified cry, and a sudden burst of bitter hopeless weeping. Hagiwara flung himself on his face, clutching with his hands and crying on the name of Buddha. It did not drown the sound of her pitiful sobbing as O-Yoné led her away.

The next night she came again, and the night after. But on the third night O-Yoné came alone, and not to Hagiwara. Rousing Tomozo from his sleep, she bound him with curses so terrible and so potent a fear that the old man swore to do her bidding. And when the darkness fell again, and Tomozo spread his master's *futon* on the floor, a single scroll was gone from the lattice above his head, and the image of the Buddha had been slipped from the folds of his girdle. Worn out and over watched, Hagiwara flung himself down, and the invocation of the Buddha died on his drowsy lips. Before midnight he was sound, so sound that when the light of the peony lantern fell on his face, he stirred and held out his arms without waking from his sleep. In the morning they found him dead, with that which had been the body of O-Tsuyu-san beside him. At his feet stood the peony lantern: it had gone out.

The following translations have been used: the *Ko-Ji-Ki*, translated by Professor Chamberlain for the Asiatic Society; his fragment of the 'Botan-Doro'; supplemented by Lafcadio Hearn, *In Ghostly Japan*; and the translations of Japanese street-songs in Hearn's *Gleanings in Buddha-Fields*. (Author's note.)

Notes

'seven valleys [and seven seas]': The parenthetical inclusions represent portions of the original typescript which were omitted from the printed version.

'Even Pass of Yomi': The entrance to Hades (in Japanese).

'*Mein süsses Lieb*...': 'My sweet love, when you in the grave, / in the dark grave will lie'. Misprints in this quotation have been corrected.

'*Wir beide bleiben…*': 'We both remain in the vault, / I lie in your arms.'
'Izanagi and Izanami': The order of the names has been corrected here.
'*hatamoto*': Direct retainer(s) of the shogun.
'*hokku*': The old name for haiku (lit. 'opening verse', of a sequence). Waddell undoubtedly took this one from Basil Hall Chamberlain's classic essay on the 'poetical epigram', as he called it:

Alas! The noon convolvulus,
That neither dew may aught avail!

The verse is by Yokoi Yayū (1702–83), and Chamberlain provides explanatory notes. The flower in question is *hirugao*, or Japanese hedge bindweed (*Calystegia japonica*), which is light pink. It is a wild convolvulus, but the same plant as the much cultivated morning glory, though it blooms later in the day. The essay first appeared in the *Transactions* of the Asiatic Society of Japan, which Waddell probably possessed. But see Chamberlain's *Japanese Poetry* (London: John Murray, 1910), pp. 248–9.

'Feast of the Bon': See the notes for 'Kwannon of the Single Grace'.
'*geta*': Wooden sandals, as above.
'*hakama*': Divided skirt-trousers, as above.
'*sama*': A polite form of address appended to a name; a more respectful form of *san*.
'*andon*': Paper lantern, as above.

Appendix: Japanese Poetry

Although Helen Waddell never wrote the essay on Japanese poetry that she alludes to in her letters to Dr Taylor, some of her ideas for it went into the reviews that she published in the *Nation*. One of these reviews has been appended below, for the insight that it gives into her thinking. Altogether Waddell appears to have reviewed four of Waley's books for this journal: his first two volumes of translation from the Chinese; then the book below; and finally his versions of Japanese Noh plays. As remarked before, Waddell and Waley were exact contemporaries, and they shared a publisher at first, though no record has yet appeared of any contact or exchange between them. This review was published on 13 March 1920.

Japanese Poetry: The Uta. By Arthur Waley
(Oxford: The Clarendon Press)

Roses, in spite of Ben Jonson and Philostratus the Athenian, smell of themselves. Like great verse, 'simple, sensuous, passionate', their own richness suffices us.

'Ask me no more where Jove bestows,
When June is past, the fading rose,
For in thy beauties, orient deep,
These flowers as in their causes, sleep'

– 'from a thick brake
Nested and quiet in a valley mild,
Bubbles a pipe:'

– 'Yet that fair field
Of Enna, where Proserpin gathering flowers,
Herself a fairer flower, by gloomie Dis
Was gathered.'

The same charm holds of violets, of honeysuckle and Madonna lilies, of most of the flowers of mid or early summer. But there are a few, spring flowers for the most part and of small substance, whose quality is nearer being magical than sensuous. The smell of roses is the smell of summer, here and now: but what of daphne flowering in the snows? That too is summer, but a summer incredibly blue and fair, somewhere in the Aegean. Flowering currant in February has the essence of August afternoons: it can turn a railway siding on the bleak Antrim coast into the Pilgrims' Road to Kamakura, pungent with the smell of pines and the hot, white bitterness of dust. A single sprig of broom – the hothouse sort – has the East of the Arabian nights in it: Baghdad, and a damsel with a figure like the letter Alif buying Othmanee quinces and peaches of Oman, jasmine of Aleppo, and water-lilies of Damascus, musk and aloes-wood and ambergris. While for narcissus – it is Homer and the fields of Asphodel. This is the charm, so tiny in content, so infinite in suggestion, of Japanese lyric.

And that charm is not only for those who remember, whose mood has been the mood of the poet. It is the charm of Japanese landscape painting: one need not have seen homing sails from a far coast, or the lighting of wild geese on a marshy plain, to find it as sure a road to the infinite as the mathematics men learned from the course of the stars. Its power is in its very indefiniteness: for there is no absolute escape in that which has a beginning and an end. The 'Ode to the Nightingale', diviner though it is than anything the East has given, runs the full circuit of a mood: begins in the inn garden at Barford on a night in mid-May, and ends there.

> 'Fled is that music: – Do I wake or sleep?'

It is perfection, but the perfection of the ellipse. Hear now this fragment from the Kokin Shu, the great tenth century anthology.

> 'O nightingale, sing on!
> Not once in the one year
> Shall spring return?'

There is neither first nor last. It rises like a single willow-branch out of spring mists: yet in three lines there is the sorrow of Prosperine's garden.

The Japanese instinct was right that chose the narrower limits of the *hokku*, after a long practice with the *tanka*. The swifter the line and the fewer the strokes, the vaster the suggestion. But when it is a matter of landscape, rather than of mood, the five line *tanka* is better; and Mr. Waley's book of *tanka* translations is a collection of Japanese prints in little. There is nothing in it to equal the best work of Basho and Buson: nothing of the strangeness of the lyric, once regarded in Japan 'as a thing almost sacred', says Mr. Yone Noguchi, 'though its dignity is a little fallen of late' –

'The old pond:
A frog leapt.
List, the water sound,'

where even the alien can feel the grey peace of the temple pond and the sudden shattering of silence: though only a Buddhist will know it for the moment of Enlightenment, the scattering of the Illusion of the world. Yet those of us who can ill afford Hokusai are grateful for these –

'The wild geese returning
Through the misty sky –
Behold, they look like
A letter written
In faint ink!'

Or this –

'On the shore of Nawa
The smoke of the saltburners,
When evening comes,
Failing to get across,
Trails over the mountain.'

Or this –

'My thoughts are with a boat
Which travels, island-hid,
In the morning-mist
Of the dim shore of Akashi, –
Dim, dim!'

Lovelier still, like a pagan rendering of the Figure seen so often in the Catacombs, this lyric on a dead child –

'Because he is young
And will not know the way to go
Would I could bribe
The messenger of the Underworld
That on his shoulders he might carry him!'

And this, loveliest and saddest of all –

'The rotten-wooded willow
At the road side
When Spring comes
Yearns bitterly for old times.'

One remembers Keats'

'In a drear-nighted December,
Too happy, happy tree,
Thy branches ne'er remember
Their green felicity.'

Set the one over against the other, if you would see in a crystal the pantheism of the East.

One is grateful to the translator, not least for the grammar and the glossary whereby he tempts the reader to share his own pleasure in the original. Yet there is somewhat against him: he should not have said of the fragments of verse in the Ko-Jiki,* the very old 'Records of Ancient Matters', 'not one is of any value as literature'. True, they are the despair of the scholars. 'This is an Incomplete Song', they say quaintly of the marvellous fragment, written by the Prince Yamato Také as he lay dying on the Moor of Nobo, returned from his last campaign –

'Ah sweet, ah sweet,
That from the hills of home
The clouds arise and come.'

They sent the Prince of Karu into exile; this is the last farewell to his wife, written as he journeyed to the islands of the South –

'No messengers there are,
I shall have gone so far.
But when you hear the crane,
Cry unto them my name,
For they my heralds are.'

Best of all, the fragment of folk-song which tells the story of the great tree whose shadow crossed the mountain at sunset, and at sunrise fell across the

*Translated by Professor Chamberlain, supplement to the Transactions of the Asiatic Society, vol. x. (Author's Note.)

islands of the bay: how it was cut down and made into a ship called Karanu – 'and a very swift-going vessel it was': how the ship was lost, and of its broken timbers some were burned for salt, and one fragment made into a lute that sounded seven miles inland from the shore. So one sang, saying:

> 'Karanu was burned for salt,
> The wood that was left they made a lute,
> The sound of it struck is the seaweed swaying,
> Rocked on the reefs in the harbour of Yura.
> The harbour of Yura bay.'

'This is a Changing Song which is a Quiet Song', say the commentators. As well they may, for it has been the lullaby of the world.

Notes

'Othmanee quinces ...': This and the next two phrases are not included in the typescript version, which is incomplete, and have been taken from the printed one. Some of the same details can be found in 'The Uttermost Isles'.

'*hokku* [haiku] ... *tanka*': The haiku is a seventeen-syllable verse in three phrases (5-7-5), while the tanka is a thirty-one-syllable verse in five phrases (5-7-5-7-7).

'Mr. Waley's...translations': In reproducing the quotations,Waddell (or her typist) somehow transmuted 'misty' in the first poem into 'wintry'. This, and a few small divergences from Waley's original punctuation, have been corrected here.

'Basho': The printed version gives 'Barho', which is obviously a misprint.

'fragments of verse': Waddell has considerably adjusted Chamberlain's originals in the *Kojiki* (Introduction, note 71) to make them more attractive and readable. For the first he has: 'How sweet! ah! From the direction of home clouds are rising and coming!', p. 271. And for the second: 'The heaven-soaring birds, too, are indeed messengers. When thou hearest the voice of the crane, ask my name,' p. 374. The typescript ends with the first quotation, so that the remainder has been taken from the printed version.

'fragment of folk-song': This and the accompanying story (like the haiku quoted here and elsewhere) are taken from Yone Noguchi's book *The Spirit of Japanese Poetry* (London: John Murray, 1914), pp. 88–9, with rather less adjustment. But the final comment shows that Waddell had also consulted Chamberlain, p. 355.